THE MOONLIGHT CHRONICLES

CHRONICLES ®

• a wandering artist's journal •

THE OUTDOOR CAMPUS
4500 S. OXBOW AVE.
SIOUX FALLS, SD 57106

"I leaned on the fountain and made a sketch of the rectory with its green gate, which I really like best, and with the steeple in the background. Possibly I've made the gate greener than it really is, and I may have made the steeple taller than it really is. All right. All that matters is that for a quarter of an hour this building was my home. Some day I will think of this rectory and grow homesick, though I just stood outside and looked at it, though I knew no one who lived in it — it will make me homesick as if it were really my home, one of the places where I was a child, happy. Because here, for a quarter hour, I was a child, and I was happy."

from Wandering
by HERMANN·HESSE

MOONLIGHT
chronicles

by
d.price

THE OUTDOOR CAMPUS
4500 S. OXBOW AVE.
SIOUX FALLS, SD 57106

TEN SPEED PRESS
Berkeley/Toronto

TEN SPEED PRESS
P.O. Box 7123
Berkeley, CA 94707
www.tenspeed.com

• Distributed in Australia by Simon and Schuster Australia, in Canada by Ten Speed Press Canada, in New Zealand by Southern Publishers Group, in South Africa by Real Books, in Southeast Asia by Berkeley Books, and in the United Kingdom and Europe by Airlift Book Co.

• Cover and interior design by Daniel Price

• Library of Congress Cataloging-in-Publication Data

• Price, D. (Dan), 1957–
   Moonlight Chronicles / [Daniel Price]
   p. cm.
   ISBN 1-58008-171-1
   1. Price, D. (Dan), 1957--- Journeys 2. Voyages and Travels. I. Title
G530.P852000
910.4---dc21   99-058200

MOONLIGHT CHRONICLES The story <u>Six Days in Hell</u> was originally published in <u>Backpacker</u> magazine.

FIRST PRINTING, 2000
Printed in Hong Kong

1 2 3 4 5 6 7 8 9 10 ~ 04 03 02 01 00

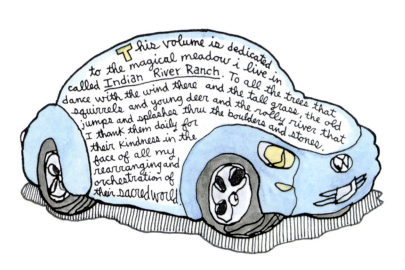

This volume is dedicated to the magical meadow i live in called Indian River Ranch. To all the trees that dance with the wind there and the tall grass, the old squirrels and young deer and the rolly river that jumps and splashes thru the boulders and stones. I thank them daily for their kindness in the face of all my rearranging and orchestration of their sacred world.

← thankyou cats...

"AcKNoWLEDGMENTs."

Thanks need to go out to JoAnn Deck and all the folks at 10-Speed Press who have helped this book get-along-little-doggie to the printer. I'd also like to thank any and all human-beans that had anything whatsoever to do with its creation and consumption.

...and my mom. →

DRAWING

...it is the best thing
that i ever do. First of
all because it gets me to be so silent.
To not be blurting out what i think about this
or feel about that. Second, I become an open
observer, jotting down visual notes about
something i see. And third, it puts me in
the world of praise. To be looking upon
an object and taking the time to sketch
it is an innocent, unaggressive, and
grounding act. It is where bliss resides.
It is pure BEING...

d.price

MOONLIGHT CHRONICLES

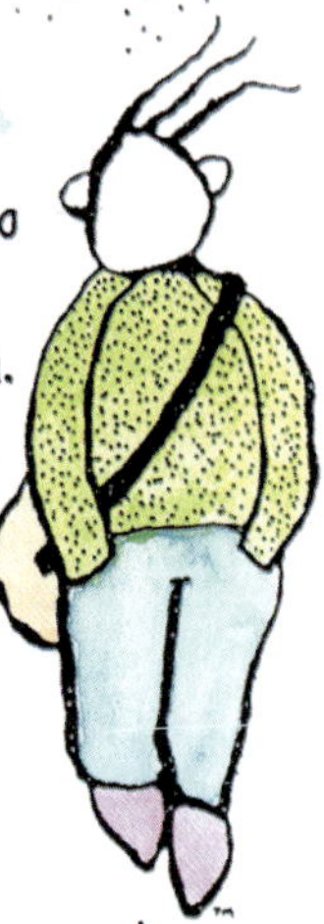

LISTEN · SEE · FIND THE WAY ·

· DRAW COOL STUFF

· HOBOS ARE FREE ·

INTRO·duck·TION

On the way home we jumped curbs and rode our bikes through mud puddles. And we drew some ducks at a pond. The wind was blowing the grass sideways.

Here's a drawing that was made one lazy day last spring. I drew the landscape and the duck on the left. My boy Shane drew the duck on the right. If you like to read and look at things that aren't too mainstreamy or are a bit odd and unusual, you may like these Chronicles. For nearly ten years I've been wandering around studying neat things like ducks and other miracles. In 1992 i began making little books of all these notes and sketches, titled it Moonlight Chronicles, and sent some out to friends. Then in 1995 a shoe company began publishing them and sent them all over the place, spreading the message of happiness via simplicity. The first 25 issues were mostly about living in a tipi, watching our kids Shane and Shilo growing up and the adventure of travelling. Now a new publisher has picked up the reins, and in addition to continuing the search for truth and beauty, they said, "Why don't you paint all the drawings?" So that's what I've been doing. It's been such a fantastic journey so far. Like finding diamonds in my dreams, only to awaken and discover that it's all diamonds, each and every little thing.

d·price

six DAYS in HELL

a walking journal by d. price

PROLOGUE

HOBO ARTIST

Five years ago, back when i was an innocent wandering hobo artist, i plunged off the east side of a place called Freezeout Saddle and walked 75 miles thru Hells Canyon. It was a tough 5 days as the stiff boots i had were torturing my feet and causing me to limp the entire way. The days were wet and long and my journal was filled mostly with complaints and only a few drawings. About the only good memory i have of that walk is finding a lonely mouse that had perished on the trail. I remember lying right down on the ground with it, looking real close and drawing each hair, every whisker.

APR 29 1999

Now I've decided to do the trip again, and this time to make a more enjoyable vagabond out of it. I've been running and doing pull-ups and push-ups for over a year, all the loose ends are tied up and I've got a very _soft_ and completely comfortable pair of boots to wear!

mouse drawn in 1994

1

SUPPLIES LIST

APR 30 1999

FOOD!

- ☑ Jerky
- ☑ Peanut butter!
- ☑ bread - deli
- ☑ dried fruit
- ☑ dry soup - pan
- ☐ Spoon
- ☑ energy bars
- several. many. lots.
- ☑ MOON PIES yum!
- ☑ cheese ← STAPLE!
- ☑ crackers
- ☐ wild eatables?
  take book
- ☐

GENERAL

pants?

- ☑ Tent
- ☑ pad
- ☑ bag
- ☐ coat (2)
- ☑ water bottles & filter
- ☑ knife
- ☑ poncho? where is it?
- ☑ headlamp
- ☐ fishhooks
- ☐ Bathroom bag (soap) T.P.

GARUDA

LOST
$40 poncho!

ART STUFF

- ☑ empty book ←
- ☑ pens
- ☑ X-Acto   colored pens?
- ☑ labels ☑ tape
- ☑ glue ☑ camera
- ☐ quotes (get panoramic)

4¾"
7 days in HELL
6½"

- ☑ whatever it is that I'll be forgetting
- ☑ map
- ☑ history book pages
- ☑ copied geology pages

2

The day i was to leave (28TH) it snowed 6 inches and made the pass, well, impassable. So i waited 2 more days in the studio, rechecking all the provisions and deciding if i couldn't leave a few more things behind. The pack and everything weighed <u>40</u>lbs. Freezeout Saddle is at <u>5,200ft</u>. So i took my snowshoes just in case. Drove to the trailhead and spoke with a camper there who said that a

Roads

↑the muddy trail to the summit →

← snow smatterings

packtrain had just left. I figured i could get thru in their tracks, so threw the snowshoes in the trunk, crawled under the pack (i only weigh 145 lbs.) and hit the trail.

It was a cool, cloudy day. Ticks in the bushes. 🕷 🕷🕷 Birds singing. Took about 2 hours and 2 Moon Pies to get to the summit. Very little snow. To the east the trail dove off 8 miles, down to the Snake River. 3

Walked down thru ever greener knolls and bluffs thinking about 3 things that I'm afraid of, and every one of them is in Hells Canyon! BEARS, RATTLE-SNAKES, AND POISON IVY.

I tied a small bell to my pack, so that would alert any bears that I was coming down the trail. I have total X-RAY vision when it comes to seeing even tiny leaves of poison ivy, so i would tip-toe around ALL of that. But the Rattlers i wasn't too sure of. Wasn't planning on sleeping on any rockpiles though, and i had a nice, long, copper-tipped walking stick that my boy and i

after the long hard winter, all these greens are SHOCKING!

where Saddle Creek meets the Snake River

4

had made, so i figured that might keep the buggers at bay.

Arrived at the Snake River late afternoon, amid beautiful Tennessee Walking horses owned by several bear hunters from Tillamook, Oregon. Their group comes in for 2 weeks every year, according to Wes, who came by later to shoo his grazing steeds away from my tent. The hunters all had big L.L. Bean tents set up next to an old hayrake. The river roared below.

Ethel Wilson who moved to the remote Saddle Creek Ranch in 1915 with Pete Wilson. They both raised cattle and hay there until 1937. In the meantime they raised eight kids.

Forest

And right at twilight, just like i remembered from the first trip, the canyon wrens came out, darting and diving in the cool air, eating bugs that were rising off the river.

Found 2 big, fully blooming lilac bushes nearby. Hung a large mass of them in the doorway of the tent and was taken back to my childhood days of baseball and lawn mowing with every whiff.

Spent the evening reading the geology and history books I'd brought along. Counted <u>3</u> Moon Pies remaining.

Idaho trail

Across on the Idaho side i saw the Hiltsley cabin at Bernard Creek. Archeologists have recovered 7,000-year-old Indian evidence and pictographs there. Bill Hiltsley built the cabin in 1901 and stayed until 1915.

edge of the SNAKE RIVER

lots of
SNAILS
on the
TRAILS

Awoke to the sound of little yellow birds singing near the tent. There were 2 or 3 raindrops that had fallen, so i quickly hopped up, packed everything and walked north, into the rocky, yawning abyss. Day two is always a bitch as you feel the pack pulling and rubbing at hips and shoulders. Chewed the inner bark of some Red Willow for the pain.

Had just planned on quietly walking the entire day, but as i came upon Bernard Creek, Mark's Creek, and significant land- slides i kept stopping to pull out the geology and history books of the area. Nearly every level spot had some- one on it at one time trying to scratch out a living.

Still hadn't seen any hikers on the Idaho side by lunch, which i ate near a rock shelter at Sluice Creek.

some canyon flowers i found →

7

Down at Pony Creek there's a big gulley that has exposed all the many land slides the area has experienced. About one foot down from the surface was a white powdery layer that was deposited 6,000 years ago when Mt. Mazama blew. (That's Crater Lake in central Oregon.) And it got me to thinking about the native people who were living here at that time. Hunter-gatherer people who awoke to find their entire world covered in a foot of white ash! What did they do? How did they survive that catastrophe? And here we modern-dayers complain

about a little rain?!

Looking west up
into the green hills
i could see Hat Point
lookout tower rising
above the trees and
snowy cliffs. The
trail meandered
around the benches
covered in tall, wet
grasses. The river
quickly flowed by
and i kept imag-
ining how easy
this trip would
have been in a
nice long, sleek
kayak. Covered
12 miles and
set up the tent
just south of a
place called Temper-
ance Creek Ranch
when the rain hit.
It's a great feel-
ing to climb in-
side the dry and

5 PM

2 cow boys, 3 mules and a black dog weathered out the rainstorm in the tiny cabin at Myers Creek, then rode away playing harmonicas in the evening light.

cozy tent with all those raindrops falling, tink, tink, just outside that thin skin. After all that firsthand experiencing of the day, the quiet closed-in tent is a perfect place to gather your thoughts, rest your body, and finish up sketches.

Saw a baby rattlesnake on the trail earlier and also lots of archeological markers at rock shelters. Looks like someone is planning on digging these sites in the future. At one place, way back under a ledge, i saw a recently excavated hole about 2 ft. square by 1 ft. deep. I did a little sifting and found this old brown bone that appeared to have been broken with a rock. Had some ancient hunter sucked the marrow from this bone?

5.1.99 PONY CREEK rock shelter

So i spent most of the rest of that day thinking about the prehistoric people who used to live in amongst all that rock and river. They would wander along the edges, searching for food, staying in their series of rock shelters each night. And they wouldn't have been able to conceive of all our modern-day ways. Of felling the big trees and sawing them up with shiny mechanical devices and creating such huge homes of concrete, steel, and wood. Humans

jet boat fisherman with white dog

lived for many thousands of years in rock overhangs, caves, and dugouts.

And then i thought long and hard about what an actual life like that would be. Primitive man would have had a much purer existence, interested mainly with being in the moment at hand. Whereas modern man is not content with just being, he feels compelled to constantly be doing something, must, as they say, make something of himself. As if a self wasn't already something quite extra-ordinary. I'm sure primitive man probably never thought that way. There were no "famous" cave men (or women), no "distinguished characters." I'm sure they just simply lived and died and spent lifetimes in the sacred presence of nature. All these thoughts and more i had sitting there in my ultra-high-tech shelter, wearing pants and a coat spun from recycled plastic pop bottles! Bizarre.

← dead mouse found on trail near JOHNSON BAR. A little red bug was get-ting ready to eat him.

raccoon tracks

Things i remember from the day: stripping naked and doing a scrub down at noon in Sluice Creek. Waving at hikers across the river at Sheep Creek. Getting to wear the Tevas for most of the day until the tall grass finally cut my toe. Lying back against the rock cliffs eating Moon Pies with the pack still on. MOON PIE COUNT 2

11

some of the
WILD FOODS
I've been eating.

white inner bark ↓

for the headache
RED WILLOW

yellow flowers

DOCK LEAVES
chews like tobacco in your cheek

BISCUIT ROOT
potato-like. old indian staple.

MINER'S LETTUCE
just like store bought lettuce!

WATER CRESS
very peppery and zesty

STINGING NETTLE
boil leaves and stalks twice in fresh H2O, just like spinach!

12

took this three and Idaho

Awakened once again by birdsong and rain. Gray skies. Low clouds. Spent entire morning slogging along through the drizzle. Ten miles on a trail that had not seen any maintenance for many years. Between Temperance Creek and Pittsburg Landing were many points of interest. Up on Suicide Point the Nez Perce Indian Chief Half Moon fell to his death. Bud and Helen Wilson ran 4,800 sheep at Big Bar for 35 years. A school-house at Two Corral Creek was run from 1908-20. And the geology shows huge alluvial fans and sediment flows from a section known as the Cougar Creek Complex. There's rhyolite, quartz

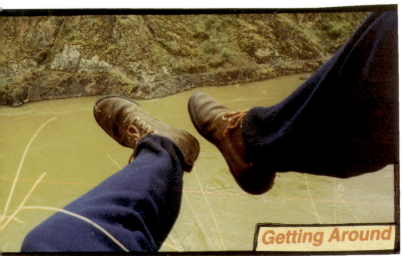

Getting Around

photo to show how wet my boots were on day to also show how close to the river the trail sometimes got.

the MOUNTAINS above PITTSBURG LANDING

diorite, plus rare meta-sediments and lavas. Mostly i found the geology book too academic and enjoyed the history book more, although the Pittsburg area was said to be one of the most diverse geographically, with tons of major happenings all crammed together.

The trail continued on as a river of grass, weeds, poison ivy, and small bushes. I considered it all one long river because the wetness soaked boots, socks, and pants to the knees. Those dirty socks were getting the scrubbing of their lives in those 2 mini washing machines called shoes. My dad had warned me that wet feet cause blisters, but by noon my feet seem fine, although quite pruney.

14

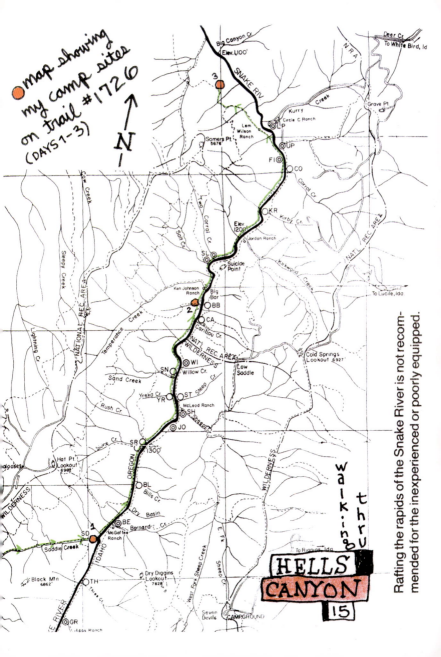

map showing
my camp sites
on trail #1726
(DAYS 1–3)

N

Rafting the rapids of the Snake River is not recommended for the inexperienced or poorly equipped.

walking thru

HELLS CANYON

15

Breakfast of Champions!

Had lunch inside a huge metal building at Pittsburg Landing. Found wood and paper so built a <u>BIG</u> fire to dry things out. Made split pea soup. And then it happened. Without warning and as quick as lightning. The first real calamity of the trip. Without even a thought about my current situation, let alone the dreadful days ahead..... i gobbled down my <u>last</u> and very precious <u>MOON PIE</u>! At first i was devastated. Then a voice of reason shone thru. And it said over and over again this one Universal Truth, "Man does <u>not</u> live by Moon Pie alone!" And so i walked on, the sad, forlorn hobo, into the rain, dejected and reduced to eating the jerky, peanut butter and celery, and dried fruit that was always intended as simply backup rations....

I may have indeed experienced my own personal hell back there in that metal barn, but that afternoon i certainly experienced the <u>hell</u> of Hells Canyon.

Stopped in at the house at Temperance Creek. It is no longer a sheep ranch, but serves as a B & B for travellers. 2 women from Steamboat Springs, Colorado, were inside debating what to wear on this rainy day. Outside in the yard there's a pipe wagon, 4 tractors, a hay baler, one grain elevator, a small Caterpillar and one hay wagon. In 1886 Tom Warnock moved 275 horses to this remote place and farmed into the 1900s.

Imagine if you will hiking up a long steep spine of a hill, 1,500 ft above the river, in the rain and coming upon a weed-choked and poison ivy-filled gully. Dead and burnt trees standing mournfully all around, with no apparent path thru it all to the pretty, grassy knoll beyond. Finally

SOMER'S CREEK CABIN
each roof piece is a 4x8 sheet of plywood. The bed in this place would only fit a midget.

getting up my nerve, i forged ahead, one tiny step at a time, finding a circuitous route to the center, which featured a huge, slimy, black mud bog. Once thru all the poison ivy you arrive on the far side with mud practically to your knees, wondering if you're going to begin itching anytime soon, (did you know that one teaspoon of poison ivy juice could give a rash to every American person?) and look up to see the longest, steepest, baby-steppingest trail in the entire canyon. When i reached the top, sweating like a dog, i pulled out the map and was pleased to discover this little piece of real estate is known as Pleasant Valley!

Reached the 12-mile goal for the day and popped up the 3,200 feet the canyon. That my knee had

* have been following these boot prints for 2 days

damp tent at looking down on night i discovered swollen up and looked

[17]

Water

on the way out of Pleasant Valley with Pittsburg L

→ just about like a red peach. The rain was never end
sounding like a christmas tree thrown on a fire.
And little puddles were forming in the corners. Still
i was dry and warm, saving a clean pair of socks
for evenings spent in the tent. Ah yes, the tent.
my refuge from the storm. Once you're deep
into a trip, you can sit in the silence of your shelter
while thinking of..... nothing. Made me realize
how <u>busy</u> my supposed <u>simple</u> life really was
back home. Only when out and about, away from
that dastardly phone and
endless projects can a
person really live like a
<u>vagabond</u> artist.

Hells Canyon Dam (Oregon).
Dam, completed in 1968, is 22 r
Oxbow off Oregon State Hwy 8
feet high and 1,000 feet wide, th
ate up to 540,000 kilowatts of e

18

"...the sense of having one's life needs at hand, of traveling light, brings with it intense energy and exhilaration. Simplicity is the whole secret of well-being."

PETER MATTHIESSEN
the Snow Leopard

far below.

found a whole pile of these along the trail.

← flowers fared well in the back pages of the empty journal.

on
of
330
ener-

19

Didn't see any mountain Goats, but did hear lots of rock fall when near cliff areas. They must have been hiding...

MAY 03 1999
DAY FOUR

○ temp. <u>40°</u>
○ condition of knee <u>swollen</u>
○ temperament- <u>nervous</u>
○ teeth brushed ☑
○ H₂O <u>1 quart</u>

Wow! The tent floor was soaked the next morning. Can see new snow on hills 500 feet above my camp. Decided to make a run (well limp) towards the pass, so quickly packed, lashing the soaking, dishrag-like tent to the outside.

Over the pass an hour later and down Somer's Creek i go. The path is about 1-foot wide, 10-inches deep and very muddy. At one point i decide it's lots easier to skate down it like a cross-country skier. Near the bottom of the canyon were 2 areas so clogged with poison ivy that i had to climb up and around on the steep side hills.

This routine of watching each and every step, using the walking stick to brush the grass and poison ivy aside, made for a several-hour <u>full-attention</u> endeavor. The second my mind wandered, down I'd go into the mud.

Chukar
old world species. Game bird. Red legs.

Once in the bottom lands i attached the bell to the pack, so as not to surprise any bears on the brushy trail. By noon i was so sick of the poison ivy i was half wishing a bear, or cougar, or something would come and chase me out of that mess. Soon i was surrounded by many wildflowers in a big meadow. The sun came out and i fell in the grass and napped for awhile while my gear hung in the bushes to dry. (see photo) →

Before long the rains returned so i stumbled on down to the river 2 miles below. With 7 more miles to go to reach that day's goal, i munched an energy bar and walked north, vowing to throw away my running shoes once i got home and take up quiet, peaceful meditation instead. Ever since

Getting There

the old horse-drawn plow sits idle at the BLANKENSHIP RANCH on Cat Creek. I was trying to imagine the events that led up to it being abandoned there in mid furrow. An accident perhaps or family illness that sent them down the river to Lewiston, never to return again?

21

i was just a little shaver my knees have sounded like pepper grinders. Obviously my year of running had only made them worse and in the mean time erased how many years off the end of my walking days.

LUNCHTIME Somerie Creek 60°

I'm pretty sure these were the FLOWERS i was lying in →

After lunch the trail stayed fairly level and close to the river. I saw many chukars flying up in pairs on nearly every corner. One couple didn't flutter up and i was able to see all their intricate feather markings. Also saw one very bright yellow bird on a fence post that tilted its head back to sing and showed no fear whatsoever. Saw tons of beetles. Strange looking and quite persistent silvery flys. Low-flying black bees. 6 Canadian geese going up river. 3 ducks lazily floating down river. 2 jumpy lizards. One rabbit under a barn. One big yellow fish leaping out of the river twice. Only one tick. Lots of snails. Coyote tracks and gun shots. (It's <u>bear</u> season.)

DRYING STUFF OUT TIME

It was difficult to get any artwork done with the poor weather. And i was very surprised to be limping along and nursing a sore appendage like i had on the last journey. If all went well and i could go up and over 2 more passes that totalled 12 miles, i would be at Dug Bar, which is where the road is. Which is where i could hitch a ride out to get my car, which was sitting all alone 50 miles upriver. A good friend of mine was supposed to be tending cattle and staying at the small ranch house there. I could begin to envision hearty hellos, <u>HOT</u> showers, and possibly even a <u>STEAK</u> dinner or two.

The beauty of Hells Canyon's vegetation can be deceiving. Nothing presents a more deceptive appearance than the refreshing, bright green of poison ivy with its white berries. <u>Beware!</u> The banks of rivers and side streams at low elevations can be dense with this poisonous three-leaved plant.

23

The geology book says these formations are pillow basalt breccia.

Only a little rain fell that night. I could hear Roland Creek Falls just outside the tent door. The wind had blown the tent dry and my sleeping bag was warm. To reduce the swelling on my knee i wrapped it in a cold wash cloth several times and just lay around all evening. At twilight i saw sunlight come blazing thru under the deep cloud cover, lighting up the Idaho hills and terraces across the river. By staring hard at the distant horizon i could see the slow movement of that enormous cloud-filled sky over the still landscape. I sat spellbound by the shear immensity of weather patterns, how they can drench hundreds of miles of the earth in just a few short minutes.

As always, it was good to be out in the wilds, wandering down some old lonely trail like some lost drifter on the wind. Habitating the creek sides or some exotic grassy hill. After several days you begin to align yourself with the rhythm

the headlamp makes it possible to stay up late writing and drawing.

of the nature all around you. No longer dreaming of pizzas or all those great movies you're missing. Just content to be a quiet observer, being in awe of it all, and <u>that alone</u> being enough to satisfy your soul. I do admit now though that I was missing those darn

3 old bottles and a Tony Lama boot found at <u>DORRANCE RANCH</u> bunkhouse

Moon Pies in a really, really bad way. A serious addiction was revealed to me that night and i dreamt i was in a Moon Pie factory being offered all of the scrumptious little buggers i could eat!

BEST PART of DAY Seeing bunches of canyon grass roll sideways in the gusts of wind that almost

25

On the last day, high above the river i saw 30 elk eating on the green hillsides. They heard my bell and all curiously watched, then ran up and over the hill.

trail ↓

toppled me over, pack and all.

WORST PART of DAY Sitting in the weeds under the soaked parka during a downpour, directly above the cabins at Copper Creek. Wondering if i should go down and get a warm, dry room for the night. (I did ask the burly attendant after the rain stopped. He said they were $200 a night! So i walked on.)

DAY FIVE MAY 0 4 1999 have to tell you that I'm no fancy equipment buyer and that my food bag, which was the <u>tent stuff sack</u>, had by this time pretty much cremated my supplies. The crackers had become a sack of powder and salt. The cheese a smoldering mass of goo. The jerky was looking more like bacon bits and the chocolate trail mix?... long gone, devoured on some forgotten treeless Tibetan-like steppe.

↑ mini fern from some canyon

↳ Balsam Root blossoms

← from way back on Freezeout Saddle.

27

Rolled out of the bag the next morning and didn't see any rain falling. The night wind had dried out everything, even my boots were looking somewhat thirsty. Saw a bunch of red pictographs at a nearby dugout, then wandered up the trail past a sign that said <u>DUG BAR</u> → <u>3 MILES</u>. "3 miles," i mumbled to myself, "what a piece of cake. No problem!" But those last three miles proved to be some of the most difficult of all. Let me explain....

As if all those past gullies of poison ivy hadn't been enough, the canyon i

deer tracks↓

was now entering was extremely narrow and obviously had just experienced a flood of some kind. Instead of there being some nice smooth and pine needle-covered trail that i could happily limp up, there was no trail at all, and tons of the dreaded ivy. At one spot i bent over to grab a handful of splendid watercress and one of those almost dry boots went

28

Splashing into the creek bed up over the ankle. Some how i managed to dance around all the poison

Open water sources are easily contaminated by human or animal waste. Water from springs, lakes, ponds, and streams should not be drunk without proper treatment. A recommended method of treatment is to bring clear water to a rolling boil for 5 minutes. Water can be scarce during dry months in parts of the NRA; carry extra water.

plants and eventually broke out above in green, sunny meadows. I drew a huge black bug and talked with 2 quiet cowboys who were leading a pack string up into the hills for some bear hunters who were due in the next day. Just as they headed out a big hailstorm hit. In sweeping gusts the sun was replaced by large

PACK STRING before the hail storm.   29

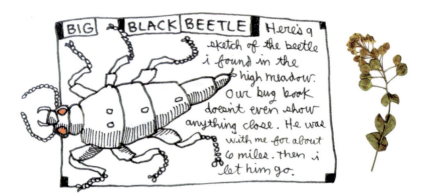

BIG BLACK BEETLE Here's a sketch of the beetle i found in the high meadow. Our bug book doesn't even show anything close. He was with me for about 6 miles. then i let him go.

pea-sized hail that bounced wildly in the grass and stung my bare arms. I retreated to a rocky overhang just east of the trail and sat munching stale nuts watching the landscape slowly turn white.

Soon the storm passed and a warm wind blew in melting the accumulated hail. The path was at first slick then started to stick in big globs to my boots. Then i came to a hillside trail that had <u>knee</u>-deep, hoof-sized, muddy holes from one side to the other! Astounded at this strange and difficult section i carefully splashed and slid down through it, cussing

the fact that horses are allowed to tromp all over this wilderness, but they won't let the mountain bikers in. Grrrr!

Rounding a corner and not at all in the finest of moods, i swear to god there sat a sparkling and wholly unopened can

30

of Coca-Cola! "It must have fallen out of that pack train", i thought as i quickly popped the top, saluted the canyon and the cowboys and the river far below with it, then guzzled.

Just then the ranch house at Dug Bar came into view so i slipped and slid the remaining 1/2 mile down, dropped my pack at the door and got under a HOT shower! → My buddy was up in the hills mending fence so i decided to take to the road and begin a whole other adventure of trying to get back to the car by hitch-hiking on the loneliest and most dead-end road in Oregon. But that's a whole other story to be told another time. There's cowboys in it too, and more rain and an old gal in a knee brace and a Cadillac, and sun and wind and eagles and Indians and fishtraps. → Life is like that, you know. Just one, long, sensuous, never-ending story.

the end

d. price
MAY 12 1999
walked 85 mi

in·ter·im, 1 ĭn'tẽr-ĭm; 2 ĭn'tẽr-ĭm, *n.* An intermediate season; intervening time; interval.

There's plenty i could tell you about here. After that long walk through Hell's Canyon, i limped around like some old man for over 2 weeks, thinking I'd maybe ruined my skinny little knee for life. But all that shuffling around was actually good because we're all going too darn fast anyway and slowing down got me to doing only the necessary and important stuff. The rest gave me a chance to read thru all 25 backissues of these <u>Chronicles</u>, and what an eyeopener that was.

Also finished up the final details of that new book i made called <u>How to Make a Journal of Your Life</u>. Cleared brush in the meadow, seeded in a new lawn and built a small cold-frame for lettuce and carrots. Helped Lynne with some of her garden projects, and Shane with his homework. Shilo's 14 now and is kinda hard to do things with. Mostly she writes in her journal, talks on the phone and needs rides to all her activities. Life..... DRAW COOL STUFF

B U T T E R F L Y

TEN WAYS TO SIMPLIFY YOUR LIFE

1. Put your radio and T.V. in the closet for several months and realize you were very addicted to their noise. Listen to silence.

2. Drink only filtered or distilled water. No more coffees, teas, milk, juice, beer or wine. Feel the pure water cleanse your body.

3. Read each night by candle light and come to appreciate what our ancestors had to make by hand in order to have nightime activities.

4. Explain to the children that the family car is not a taxi and that bicycles are a great non-polluting way to get around.

5. Walk several more steps to the bathroom and use the toilet paper to blow your nose. Never buy a box of Kleenex again.

33

A MEMORIAL
DAY·WEEKEND·CRUISE

Map labels: ASTORIA, HOOD RIVER, COLUMBIA RIVER, THE DALLES, ARLINGTON, PENDLETON, JOSEPH, LAGRANDE, PORTLAND, TILLAMOOK, CORVALLIS, EUGENE, PACIFIC OCEAN

72° SUNNY

Lynne is my partner and mother of our two children. When we first got together way back in 1975, she was always involved in dance and over the years since performed in many dance troupes. Her lifetime dream has always been to see Mikhail Baryshnikov live and this weekend he is appearing at a big concert hall in Portland. She has 2 tickets. She invited me to go, so after the kids got out of school on Friday off we went.

It's a big holiday weekend and everyone's cars are totally loaded down with fun gear. One family's jeep had their raft come off at 65mph! We drove west into the pine covered hills and down the old winding road that runs above the freeway into Pendelton. Saw a whole

FORD

BEGIN MILEAGE 20,932

34

3PM

line of clothes blowing sideways in the wind. Got Shane to draw the water tower or whatever it is in Boardman. We talked about how ridiculously huge the camping trailers are becoming these days. Nearly as big as semi-truck trailers!

While Shilo was sleeping in the back seat with headphones on, Shane and I gazed at the passing scenes. We saw a lone black crow walking down a railroad track. We saw a forest of Erector-set-like power lines emerging from a nearby hydroelectric dam and heading for the big cities to the west. Shane counted 130 train cars running fast on the Washington side across the Columbia River.

Arrived at our favorite campsite near Biggs but found all the spaces taken. On a lark i drove up a canyon into the hills high above the river looking for a secluded spot to camp at, but all we saw up there was endless fields of wheat rolling in the stiff wind. The tiny town of Wasco didn't have any motels so we drove back down to the freeway and on into the evening sunset and a 1930's Motor Motel in the Dalles. Before going off to sleep Shane sat up with one of those stark kid realizations and said, "Hold it, haven't a bazillion people slept about a in this bed?" So we explained to him how the good maids come in to

Before

35

change the bedding on a daily basis. "But still...."
he said.

MAY 26 1999 I can't even remember what we had for breakfast, or if we even did. By 9AM we were rolling along on the Columbia River Scenic Byway. Curving up into the flowering hills and through ancient basalt lava flows. We flicked bottle caps off the Rowena Crest rest area, giving them the flight of their lives, twirling down into the green carpet of oak trees far below.

my two favorite buildings are on this road.

Later on that morning we chugged (the car developed an engine problem), into the town of Hood River. Pulled out the old camera and shot a few wind surfer pictures. One of the riders said that the end of May was the beginning of the season here, and that from now on the winds would be steady. And then off he went, out into the wind lashed waves to dodge barges and skim at high speed across all that blue, cold water.

its neat to see how far ahead all the growth is here compared to our mountain valley home.

36

7:30 PM Once in Portland, Lynne's pronouncement that we had Grandad's little house completely to ourselves, was greeted with hearty applause. The kids pillaged the fridge and cupboards for sweets while Lynne and i showered and got all duded up for the <u>BIG NIGHT</u> out!

And don't forget that this experience was one that Lynne had been waiting on for <u>23</u> years. Who knows why but just the mere mention of the name <u>Baryshnikov</u> would get her all wobbly in the knees and starry eyed. And whenever I'd try to question her she'd just begin going on and on about how high he could jump, (I'll get a trampoline) or the size of his thighs (Hey, I'll push some weights or take steroids). I'll tell ya, it was enough to make a guy get those old green nasties. The jealousy thing, you know. But i hung in there, knowing every woman must have her fantasies. And even if i couldn't leap as high or gesture as beautifully with the wave of a hand, i could still fish pretty good and draw and write to boot. And i could provide for my family, and, and, oh fiddlesticks.....

ROSE AT GRANPA'S PLACE

37

at the theatre i snapped a quick picture of this man who had a white parrot on his arm. He was greeting all us folks near the entrance and seemed to know everybody.

The kids were all set up to stay at the house watching a movie called <u>The Fly</u> and Lynne and i rushed down the old Banfield Freeway into the sparkling city. Lynne was dressed in a long, flowing black gown, black shoes, and silver earrings. The man who took our tickets was funny and told us a story about a guy who left his Visa card in the ticket envelope, so now he always asks the concert goers to please remove their tickets from the envelopes. "Not that i don't <u>LOVE</u> spending other people's money", he joked.

We were somewhat early so i bought us two dark and potent beers that we drank while sitting on a red velvet loveseat watching the elegant crowds, the amazing chandeliers hanging from gilded and very ornate ceilings. Soon a soft bell chimed and we all ushered ourselves into the enormous hall with the stage quiet and serene far below. There were four dances in all. Not ballet, but strange and evocative modern dances that involved, as far as i could figure, about <u>10</u> different body postures and movements, choreographed in any number of <u>different</u> combinations. All in all it didn't get me too excited.

THE MAN

Not like seeing a cast of fabulous circus aerialists or the Riverdancers would. But when i looked over at Lynne she seemed quite mesmerized and only at the end of it all did she mumble something about wishing she had seen him back during his ballet days. She really wanted to see if we couldn't somehow meet and shake his

39

CITY CENTER PARKING
LOT-143
201 S.U. SALMON & 2ND.
PORTLAND, OREGON
Lot No.: 143

Ticket Purchased At:
12:59p May 29, 1999

Visa:
Card Charge: 4237-103
Total Paid: $ 3.00
$ 3.00

Receipt #: 00280

PLACE TICKET FACE UP
ON DASH! MANAGEMENT NOT
RESPONSIBLE FOR LOST
OR STOLEN ARTICLES!!
****

and the other dancers' hands, but as we neared the lower section doors leading to the stage we were confronted by two bulldog-like ushers who obviously had no intention of letting anyone past.

We then wandered out into the chilly night and stumbled upon the stage door exit where a big group of autograph seekers gleefully waited. "Ah hah!" said Lynne and we joined in the crowd watching as various musicians and a few dancers emerged. After about 30 minutes Baryshnikov appeared and very wearily signed everyone's programs. Lynne said she made eye contact with him and said,

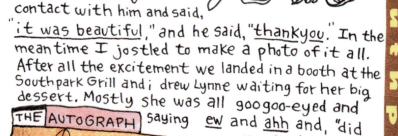

new earrings

fish net sweater

new black dress

"it was beautiful," and he said, "thankyou." In the meantime I jostled to make a photo of it all. After all the excitement we landed in a booth at the Southpark Grill and i drew Lynne waiting for her big dessert. Mostly she was all googoo-eyed and saying ew and ahh and, "did you see how short he is?" She was just like a little kid. Very content and awfully happy.

THE AUTOGRAPH

Southpark

LYNNE'S SALAD

DAN'S APPLESAUCE
AND STRAWBERRIES

SHANE'S EGGOS
AND SAUSAGES

SHILO'S POTATOES

no fork, she must have eaten that to

BIG OUR LUNCH OUT

Everytime we come to Portland we have a huge meal at the local buffet. The food is always very good tasting and you usually come away feeling <u>overly</u> full and in need of a good long walk. Today however, Lynne really went overboard and after the last bowl of sweet vanilla ice cream she just about turned <u>green</u>! So we rushed her back to grandpa's place and put her in bed while we went off shopping downtown. When we asked her how she was feeling, all she could utter was a barely audible "tight."

B R O C C O L I

the cherries on the tree out front are still green →

grandpa's little yard is very colorful

41

flowering tree

Slept in the following day until 10AM, went out for that big meal and then off to the mall with Shane & Shilo. They, like all kids nowadays, like to go into stores, and i find myself wishing that they could be just as enthusiastic about other things. I can't seem to get used to seeing them always wanting to buy more pants, and CDs and swimsuits. Especially when they already have those things. But i try not to gripe about it too much, remembering back to my own teenage days of working all summer only to blow my entire earnings on chrome wheels for my car or fancy new skis.

I just hope they can shake themselves loose of all that consumerism. It can become so overwhelmingly lethal and never ending. It can leave us feeling so empty and life becomes "planning for the next cool thing to buy."

The city is filled with very bright and blooming flowers.

42

Shane's hot chocolate

TAKE OUT

NAME The Prices having a last breakfast out on their memorial Day weekend trip. We

PHONE NUMBER can't believe Lynne is eating more food after yesterday's

TIME ORDERED 10AM Buffet experience! She got the French Toast, Bacon, and a big

PICK UP TIME Big Omelette. With O.J. YUM!

LYON'S restaurant on N.E. 122ND

MAY 27 1999

The next day was Monday and time to head the direction of home 310 miles to the east. The car sputtered along but seemed to run fairly well at top speed. All along the wide Columbia River were boats filled with

fishermen

43

anxious fishermen. The kids were reading books in the backseat. I tried to just drive along and not have any thoughts. To just see that white highway line that leads to an endless horizon.

The landscape along the river looks Martian with all the red rocks & windblown water. Not much habitation. Just pockets here & there of man's feeble and awkward attempt to tame the landscape. And us, the

consummate consumers, out speeding forever on in our enclosed capsule of comfort.

It can get you to imagining that you transported yourself to a whole other planet. That you're vacationing on Mars, or a moon of Mars, riding out across the tundra

44

in your little speedster. Soon Lynne mentions that maybe my speed is a little high and i throttle back, realizing it's the Earth we are travelling on, but still so exotic....

I OPENED my eyes upon a strange and weird landscape. I knew that I was on Mars; not once did I question either my sanity or my wakefulness. I was not asleep, no need for pinching here; my inner consciousness told me as plainly that I was upon Mars as your conscious mind tells you that you are upon Earth. You do not question the fact; neither did I.

EDGAR RICE BURROUGHS

the kids playing in a wheat field out above the Columbia Gorge.

So that's just about it for that outing. We drove thru a dusty rain the last 60 miles. I remember the valley really smelled like home. That pungent odor of bursting cotton wood leaves. And sitting by the river one late afternoon I thought back to that long weekend. I remembered a drawing i had made of an old fire hydrant that was down-town. It was Saturday i think. Shane and i were sitting in the quiet way that we do, waiting for the girls to be done shopping. And i quickly drew the hydrant. It's just a really good memory is all. Nothing too important or anything.

KENNE[DY]
150
K W
KENNEDY
ELMIRA, N.Y.

END
MILEAGE
21,650
total
driven
718 MILES

DRAWING

RIGHT HANDED

a very small mole that the cats left on the sunny back steps today. He is only about 2 inches long with his tail. Someone's going to be missing this little one when nighttime comes.

MAY 18TH

LEFT HANDED

close-up of paw.

STUFF

The kids have 5 cats here at their little farm. We have to always buy lots of cat food, but they are very companionable. We enjoy petting them and also giving the smallest one lots of flea baths. His name is MONKEY.

47

One of the gourds that Lynne grew then dried last summer

One of the neat discoveries that we made last year were these watercolor post-cards. You can buy them at most art stores. They come in a stack of 15 or so. You make a nice painting on it, stamp it, then mail it off to your buddies.

*here's one → we sent to Lynne when she was away for a week.

6 5 99

SOME of YOUR FLOWERS

direct to you from that little Raisin Ranch at end-of-the-road, Oregon.

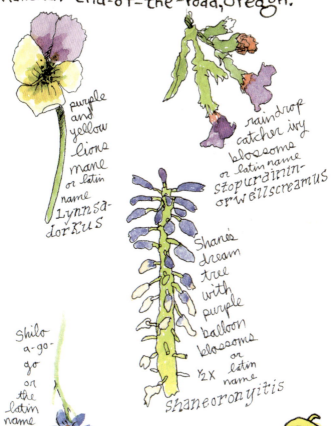

purple and yellow lions mane or latin name Lynnsadorkus

raindrop catcher ivy blossoms or latin name stopurdinin-orwellscreamus

Shane's dream tree with purple balloon blossoms or ½x latin name Shaneoronyitis

Shilo a-go-go or the latin name shilorosy

POP

* we made up our own names. Funny Ha.Ha

49

Saw this bushy-tailed creature go shuffling thru the meadow once, then saw it again a few weeks later sitting on a rock in the sun. I was clipping some bushes and noticed that the animal wasn't running off as i approached, like wild animals usually do. What it did instead was begin aimlessly wandering around in small circles, coming right up to my feet and sniffing at them. It was no longer bushy but had lots of hair missing off its hind end. Its face seemed dazed.

WOOD CHUCK

5 lbs
2 ft LONG

My first thoughts were that maybe the chemical i had used to kill the dandelions had poisoned it. Or maybe it was old, blind, and near death. I sat for a long time watching it act totally disoriented and pitiful. Then i did what i thought the animal wanted me to do. I took it upon myself to put it out of its misery and gave it a river burial. Did i do the right thing?

DOGHEAD CANOE

KNIVES

If you like knives you should call 800-251-9306 for a copy of the Smoky mt. Knife Works catalog. For the past 5 years Shane and i have been trying to build a knife collection. He likes the swords and fancy new blades best. I'm partial to the older styles. The kind that every kid carried in their jeans pocket back in the old days. Pocket knives are traded by old-timers who sit whittling on town square in the south. Knives have that feeling of a solid object in your pocket and can be used for cutting fishing line or carving slingshots. Lots of images come to my mind when i see an old pocket knife. Summer. Watermelons. Bare feet. Sunshine...

CASE CLASSIC

CASE

S P Y D E R C O

51

FIRST DAY of SUMMER

Once again Shane Boy and i are in the business of lawn mowing this summer. Lynne bought this new self-propelled mower for Shane to use. We so far have 4 different lawns that we work on. We get 10 dollars for each one and we like the work alot. Every Monday we load them up in the trunk of the old Dodge and drive across town. We like to mow because it's a thing you can do that gives you lots of good feelings. To spend a half hour or so giving the turf a good haircut, then standing back and admiring all that smooth green carpet is a wonderful feeling.

WORMS

$229.00

Ants

MURRAY

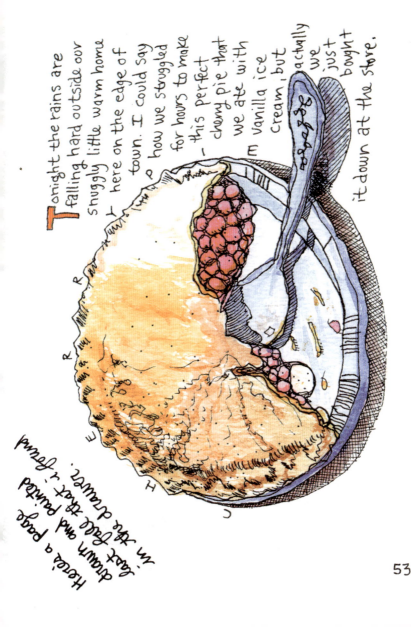

Tonight the rains are falling hard outside our snuggly little warm home — here on the edge of town. I could say how we struggled for hours to make this perfect cherry pie that we ate with vanilla ice cream, but actually we just bought it down at the store.

Here's a page that I drew and painted back in the drawer.

Last saturday we all piled in Grandpa's car and went to the local hot rod show. there were 300 exquisite old-time autos and one restored biplane. After walking thru them all, Shane and i decided that our favorite one was this '52 Mercury with flames.

chopped top

1952 MERC

I also talked with my mechanic Mike who had brought out his dad's orange 1963 drag car that they used to run in southern California. He also had an old scrapbook of photos that showed the car being raced. Mike said it took them many hours to get it all cleaned up for the SHOW.

The other night i found a $100 bill in my wallet and asked Shane to draw it:

When I started drawing this bill I thought it was kind of cool, but towards the part where I would have put Franklin in, it got a little boring, so instead I drew a dragon named Abraham Lincoln.

by: SHANE Price

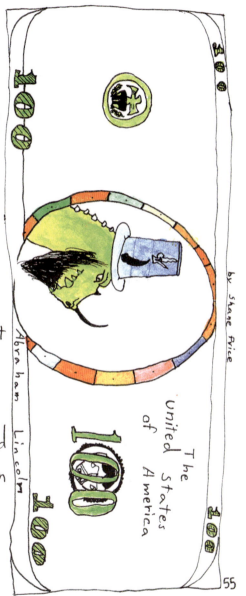

SUMMER

comes late up here in our mountain community. You can pretty much count on your new bean sprouts getting nailed by a frost most all of this month. But when the clouds do go away and that late evening light comes blasting across town, you can sit and listen and look at all the chickens milling around in the tall pasture grass. Or you can get a lawn chair and sit in the shade of the cottonwoods or up in the treehouse and close your eyes and listen real good to the sounds of planes overhead and trucks on the road, kids playing in the neighborhood and screen doors slamming and cats meowing. Maybe because our summers are so short, we savor each and every special moment we can.

JUNE 72°
ELEVEN 7 PM

A

bout one month ago i put my camera in the car's glove compartment. I thought it might make a neat series of pictures if i were to pull it out and get snapshots of all the people who i know in this county. So far I've photographed Johnny, the guy who gasses up my car, and Casey and Randy, the mechanics who work on it. Then this morning i came upon a new construction scene just a short distance from my place. Seems they are getting ready to build a brand new bridge, replacing the beautiful old art-deco one. I've wanted to draw it for years, so i sat down in the ditch and did just that. I also made a photo of it.

Hurricane Creek Road

JUN 10 1999

57

going for a little WALK in the WOODS

It's one of those crazy kind of days. The kind of day that makes me realize how overly busy i am. So darn busy that i can't meditate or just be in the moments. I get angry and sad. I wonder why i can't just go live in a tipi and draw all day.

H2O

PENS

BUSY BRAIN

CAMERA

one black ant

FIR CONE

Even though my life is simpler than most, i still have these huge cravings to just go hide out in the woods. To be living free each day in a tent next to a rolling river.

Last night as i was busy watering Lynne's lawn and trying to figure out what to feed all her visiting cousins for dinner, i looked up and saw this mt. looming so solid in the distance and i knew i needed to hike in to see it.

So i walked slowly about 3 miles in and threw rocks and sticks in the river. The deer tracks brightened my mood. This place is wild and and free. It can get you all smooth and serene again.

68

APPLE FOR LUNCH
#4020
WASHINGTON
EXTRA FANCY L&E GOLDEN DELICIOUS

One hot June afternoon
i was sweating it out on a sunny hillside. I
was helping the neighbor thatch and rake his
lawn. Later in   the day Lynne called and
said she wanted   to go car camping. By
8PM we were   all at a riverside
eden about   60 miles south.
there was   a skittish deer
that you   could throw
apple chunks
and bagel   we
pieces   found
to. A   nineteen
loud   MORELS
thunder-   at the camp.
storm rocked us to sleep and we didn't
awake until 10AM the following morning.
        The next day we sat around drawing,
playing Frisbee, rock climbing on a nearby
boulder, and eating caramels. On the way
home we stopped in a tiny town and saw
a big   thunder   / storm moving across
          the   canyons. A
          man   there gave us
                      a just Killed
                      rattlesnake.

Dragon
by
Shane

Lynne
painting

59

60

Fishin' and Hikin' and PLAYING and ridin' bikes and eatin' snake. Yass, I dug it.

16-year-old Max came to spend a week with us this summer. He liked to read books. He also made this art while we were camping.

MAX

I was noticing a tiny hummingbird racing past the studio window a few weeks ago. Then today as i was watching the meadow from the front porch, i spied it again down by the ponds. After darting around a bit it landed on the pink flamingo lawn ornament that sits near the pond. The hummingbird then rubbed its beak and tail feathers on the plastic neck. Maybe it thought the fake bird was its mother? Sometimes you can see animals do the strangest things....

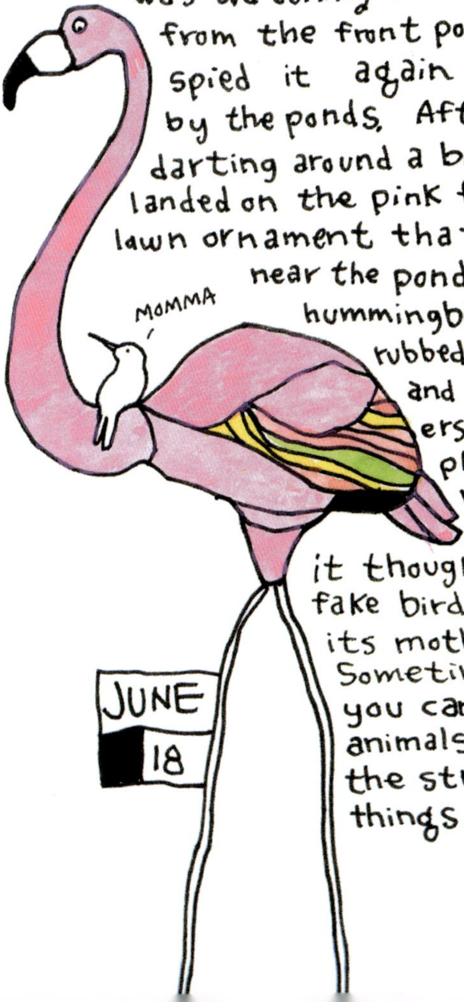

MOMMA

JUNE
18

61

drawing

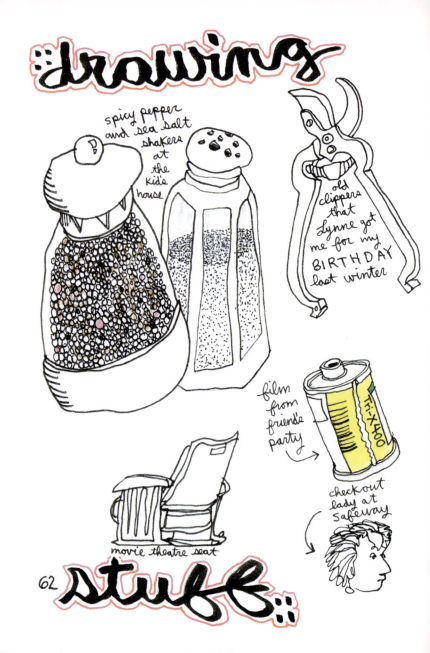

spicy pepper and sea salt shakers at the kid's house

old clippers that Lynne got me for my BIRTHDAY last winter

film from friend's party

Tri-X400

checkout lady at Safeway

movie theatre seat

62 stuff

It's always nice to be able to get a break from the kids for a bit. We've been doing the whole kid routine for the last fifteen years and sort of need a rest once in awhile. Over the years they have become our best friends and we love spending time doing things with them.

There's some tiny fish-like bugs on the top part.

WHAT ONE OF LYNNE'S FLOWERS LOOKS LIKE in HER GARDEN

Now that they have become teen-agers, things are quite a bit different. They can be moody and hard to relate to at times. We know that they are trying on different ideas so that when they do become adults they will know who they are and what they were meant to do with their life.

So we try to give them room to grow and experience the many choices they are subjected to. Sometimes it's hard when you hear yourself saying "No" several times in a row. Sometimes it's easy and things flow.

63

THINGS SEEN THIS SUMMER DAY

6AM Joseph Mt. all dark orange in the morning light.

7AM One juicy slice of homemade cherry pie disappearing from my plate.

8AM Beach Ball, our cat, crying from the inside of a silver cage at the vets.

9AM Bugs on the windshield at 60mph.

10AM An amazingly intricate quilt on the wall at the marriage counselor's office.

11AM Water, smooth and clear, gushing over huge boulders at the park.

12 NOON Lightly brown, soft and chewy macaroon cookies disappearing from a nearby carton. My sticky fingers.

1PM Heavyset man walking into the store with his helmet on. He rode up on a silver Honda motorcycle.

USM

FRIDA

64.

about six months ago we were driving home from a long day of snowboarding when we saw this old hat come flying off a speeding orange VW camper. We came to a stop and picked it off the road. It was very well worn, all scrunchy and had obviously been though many adventures. Its wild-haired owner was cruising down the road far ahead completely oblivious to its fate.

those SUMMER days are ROLLING on by.

many moons rose and fell here in our little notch in the planet. The hat hung forlornly out on the front porch, only occasionally being thrown on a small blonde head, brim pulled down tight, long strands of hair pouring out the small hole in back. Spring came and went. The solstice passed by unnoticed, too rainy for celebration. A friend and i spent weeks trying to organize a DRUM circle. Our third attempt found our group of eight gathered high on the grassy lake moraine sitting next to a big tipi as a nibbled-on biscuit moon rose in the east. One of the drummers was new, his elfin goatee blonde and round face cheery. He was talking about his orange van.... i asked had he lost an old cap.... and we became instant good friends. I could already imagine our hearty hand wavings as we passed on future curving hiways here in our small valley. 65

EVERYTHING I NEED to KNOW I LEARNed while DRAWIng

by DANNY GREGORY

FOR MY PAL, DAN PRICE

everyone can do it except those people who say they can't ● you'll Never get perfect, you'll just get BETTER ● there are No miStakes. only LESSONS ● Don't Do it for FAME or $. ● Do it FOR you ● Don't seek beauty. see it ● Everyone's idea of the perfect PEN is Different ● Learn from others, but DON'T BE an imitator ● No BOOKS and No teachers canteach you as much as Practice ● IF you DON'T Like a DRAWING, turn the Page and Do another ● always carry a PEN ● KNOW WHEN to STOP ● study how kiDS do it ● THE BESTWAY is to BE STILL ● NEVER Be too aShamed of what you DRAW ● NEVER be too PROUD either ● AVOID ERASERS ● Give your DRAWINGS away. But keep a copy ● DON'T BE JUDGEMENTAL. ugly subjects make Beautiful DRAWINGS ● CONCENTRATE ● RELAX ● HAVE FUN ●

66

LIVING WITH TWO Teen-agers!

I remember when the kids were small how people would always say, "Well they may be little angels now but just look out when they become teenagers!" Of course we never listened to that kind of talk. But after watching them slowly mature you do notice the changes. No longer do an old blanket and a few toys get transformed into a circus big top complete with imaginary lions and bears. And an innocent "Hey kids, why don't you make a lemonade stand today?" is

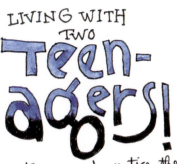

SHILO'S HAND

THE WATCH

countered with a "Yeh right Dad". So you slowly learn as a parent that no longer are you the King and Queen of your children's lives. And you come to the sad realization that they would rather go skateboarding or hang out shopping with their friends than spend the afternoon hiking or biking with you. And maybe for most parents this is a big relief, but for Lynne and i it's been like losing our best friends. And sometimes i try to explain these feelings to them, not in a bring-you-down, sad

THE MAKEUP

67

sort of way, just matter-of-factly, this-is-how-i-feel way. And i really think they understand that sadness. We always spent a lot of time in conversation with Shane and Shilo about how lucky they where to be kids and living out those kid years in appreciation for all the freedoms

THE GOOD OLD DAYS~ SPRING 1992

and silly times. How when you're a kid you can do all this cool stuff like play in grass, fish all day, or just lie around drinking Kool-Aid and running through sprinklers. Things that most adults would love to do if we didn't all walk around wearing our big coat of guilt so much. I mean why don't we just admit it, if we just went out and played all day and forgot about all our supposed concerns, we'd feel guilty as hell. So now there they go, plummeting right on into adulthood and not

68

hearing much of anything we have to say.
So i guess it's time for us both to
grow and change together. Once you've
experienced the "angelhood" of your
children's lives (see photos) it's hard
to let those images go. When you
tell your daughter repeatedly to be
home by 6PM and she keeps coming
in at 9PM, even _after_ you bought
her a _new_ watch so she always
knows what time it is, you can get
really frustrated. And then all manner
of strange kids in <u>CARS</u> begins to
show up at odd hours wondering, "Where

is Shilo?" I'll
tell ya, it's
enough to make
a parent run
out the back
door into the
garden and
just SCREAM!
Which we some-
times do. But
mostly we are
just trying to
be present and
listen to what
they say. We
really love
them a lot.

Back when i was a kid, some 3
GO-CARTS. I'd stare at a
and dream i was racing
friends. But for whatever reason
the dream of owning a cart faded
one month ago the kids and i
about 3 days   getting the   g
Then we   used a

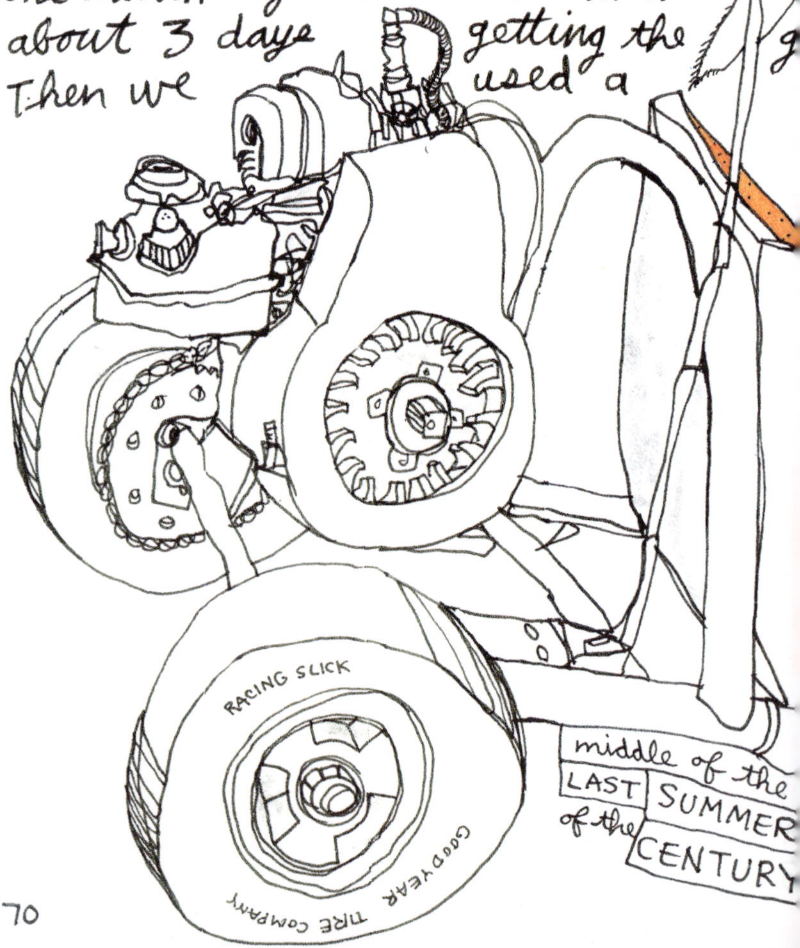

RACING SLICK

GOODYEAR TIRE COMPANY

middle of the
LAST SUMMER
of the CENTURY

lady buying a pop from a vending machine.   6PM

Sometime last spring we got to talking with my sister who lives on a country farm, about having our kids down for a week. And already that time has come. Just one day after the 4TH and Shilo's birthday and fireworks and drum circles. Six hours down thru the sunburnt landscape we drove. Over pine-covered mountains to the state's largest city. We met at a mall near a Levi's store and waved good byes thru bug-splattered windshields.

TRAIN

HEADING BACK HOME

Ancient Basalt cliffs

trucks

Sleeping Bag

Sandale

76

5:45 AM

Bird

trees

amped out on a summer-smelling hillside behind this
school at about 10PM. Millions of birds were chirping
early the next morning. Blue sky. Brown hills. The sound
of trains chugging by. Air so dry and brittle you can
taste it. It tastes like one of those long yellow
stems of dry grass you chewed on as a kid, waiting way
out in that lonely left field position for a fly ball.

77

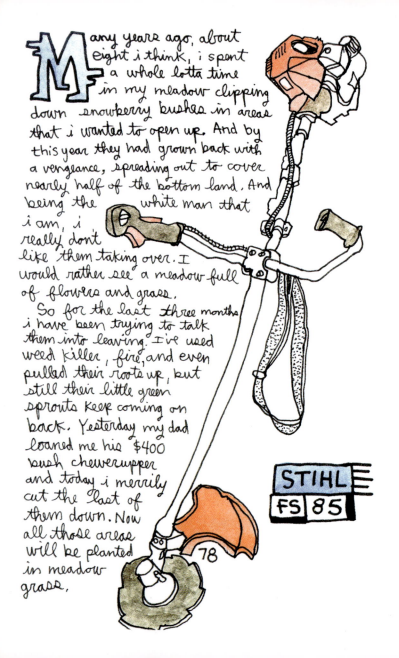

Many years ago, about eight i think, i spent a whole lotta time in my meadow clipping down snowberry bushes in areas that i wanted to open up. And by this year they had grown back with a vengeance, spreading out to cover nearly half of the bottom land. And being the white man that i am, i really don't like them taking over. I would rather see a meadow full of flowers and grass.

So for the last three months i have been trying to talk them into leaving. I've used weed killer, fire, and even pulled their roots up, but still their little green sprouts keep coming on back. Yesterday my dad loaned me his $400 bush chewerupper and today i merrily cut the last of them down. Now all those areas will be planted in meadow grass.

STIHL
FS 85

78

Now I'm no psychological expert, but I'm wondering if 9 clothespins on one of Lynne's socks means anything, seeing how Shilo hung the clothes on the line <u>after</u> she was told, "No you aren't going to the lake with your friends today!"

This last week i had to write out an actual <u>CONTRACT</u> with Shilo so that she would promise to be home each evening by 6PM for dinner. After being grounded for 2 weeks for staying out after dark, she turned right around and did it again! out to the lake with friends till 9 o'clock without even calling home. What's a parent to do?

MAD SHILO

79

Gone Fishing

a hot JULY day

Today was about 200° out and the house got so hot that we rode bikes over to fish at the pond.

quack quack

The ducks kept dunking their whole entire heads down in the water which looked cool. We were totally attacked by a bunch of blood-sucking dive-bomber bugs and the sun was long gone so we rode our bikes back down the gravel road, under an orange full moon, past barking dogs and on to home where Shilo showed me her little carnival gold-fish that had just died.

Bzzzzzz

MARR Pond

Island

By Shane

80

SHANE GETS A girlfriend?

floppy hat

the NEW BOY

bullet and mushroom necklace?

Shane's fake pile of dog crap really was a BIG hit with his mom!

can this man carry a tune?

YES ☐ NO ☐

KID ROCK

ROB ZOMBIE

Like most parents, Lynne and i are learning to adjust <u>our</u> thinking to the altogether <u>new</u> ways our teenagers are acting. But sometimes we still have to ask ourselves, are we just old-fashioned or does that ROB ZOMBIE CD <u>really</u> suck?

Now days when you walk in the house, there's a huge wall of noise emanating from the new stereo and it's really hard to not want to run over and turn it off. Then is when we try to think back to our own high school days when <u>WE</u> listened to the likes of <u>ALICE COOPER</u> and <u>KISS!</u> and even <u>BLACK SABBATH</u>, and thought they were just great. I remember hiding under the stereo cabinet most every afternoon with big bulging headphones on, blowing out those tender ear-drums. And my parents never said a word... So life goes on and it seems that sometimes it's pretty okay, then a big whopper hits. Like now Shane has a girlfriend? We can't even believe it.

81

CAMPOUT AT THE LAKE

Yesterday was another HOT one. After our lawn mowing jobs the boy and i zoomed up to the lake and jumped in the flumes below the dam, then we cleaned up our old campsite about half way around the east side and returned later that evening to camp for the night. Roasted marshmallows over the hot driftwood fire and watched the sunset turn the water pink and red and then purple, Then Shane began throwing handfuls of sand and pebbles out over the surface of the lake and it sounded wonderful, like a thousand little drums saying good night to a perfect day.

dock

fish?

big log

shane's knife

82

guess i need to tell you some more "Life with those Darn Teenager" stories. the other night Shilo came in late once again, so we grounded her for two whole weeks.

So today Shilo and i spent the entire day together. She helped with all my projects and we ate lunch at an outdoor cafe. Shilo drew the umbrella lady. and i drew the old self She was her both had again and we we a good time. that also told her in if she comes that late again she can't be on the dance team. That got her attention, boy did it ever. 83

LUNCH with SHILO ROSE

CHIEF JOSEPH DAYS

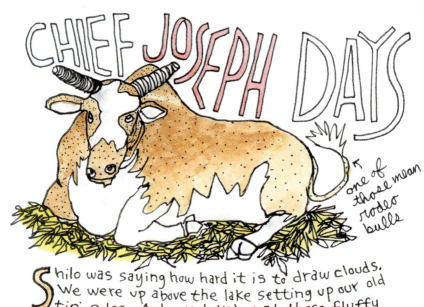

one of those mean rodeo bulls

Shilo was saying how hard it is to draw clouds. We were up above the lake setting up our old tipi poles. And we looked up at those fluffy white balls slowly flying along and both did agree that yes, clouds are hard to draw. And we sat in the dry grass up there, in the very middle of sum- this most special of sum- mers, just a few days before our little town here in the mountains becomes invaded by many hundreds of cowboy-hatted, tobacco-chewin' horse-wranglin' types. And we felt the summer sun and the wind and all those sweet smells of the season rolling over us, on down thru the pines and into the town far below.

On the way home we stopped off to see this year's bucking bulls. One of the Texas Longhorns was eat- ing peacefully, then charged at Shilo, hitting one of his heavy horns on the steel corral. Then he went back droopy eyed to eat some more hay.

The next day Shilo stayed home and Shane and i drove back up to the lake to take the tipi poles down cause we couldn't seem to find the canvas cover. He seemed very sleepy so we only sat a short time on the granite boulders, in silence, looking down at the boat-strewn, bathtub-like lake. A pickup roared by with 2 kids and a very yellow bike in the back. They were beating loudly on the top of the cab.

Before heading home to eat dinner we stopped in to watch the carnies set up all the rides and games. Shane said he could ride the wildest one 20 times and still not throw up. I said I'd probably just stick to the Ferris wheel.

Peace man!

greasy guys setting up carnival rides on Tuesday afternoon

really cool old bank of lights

85

The very next night we were back standing next to the bumper cars a good friend said, "I used to just hate to ride the Ferris wheel. Every time I did my stomach would be left dangling up in the air."

The kids rode all the rides except the Ring of Fire, which Shilo said was "too scary." And Lynne even rode a few, even after eating a long greasy corn dog.

BUMPER CAR

Mostly i sat back and watched and did a few sketches. One of the things that really gets me about carnivals is the places they are erected. One day you've just got your ordinary dusty small town street, maybe a little tuft

some cool carnival lights

SICK RIDER

86

of grass growing here and there and then BOOM, all of the sudden that boring place becomes a small city of lights, buildings, noise, people, smells, and loud generators. And a few days later POOF! it's all disappeared again and only the trampled and dead pathways in the grass testify to it all ever even being there in the first place. Like some enormous spaceship had landed to rest for awhile, then lifted off, leaving only its imprint on the soft ground.

Saturday is the big parade. We saw horses, Indians, horses, wagons, clowns, horses, princesses, horses, fire trucks, horses, dogs, more horses, and old-timer Sidney Austin who had on a huge cowboy hat.

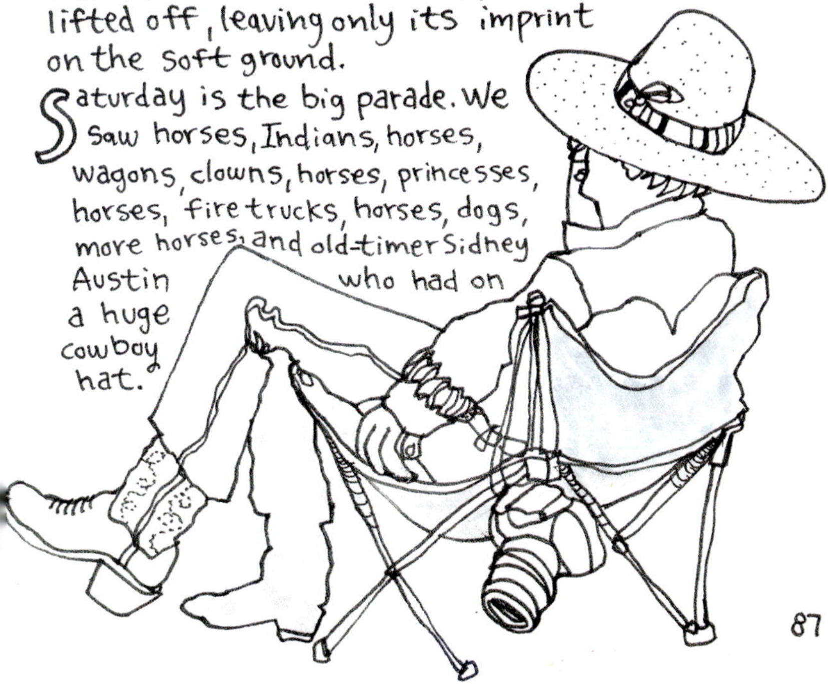

guy with wild head-dress

87

some neat stuff

small feather

Strawberries and fresh sweet peas from Lynne's garden and one pretty beat butterfly at this year's carnival.

88

BARREL RACER

RODEO

...i did mean to tell you about the rodeo. Lynne and i payed $24 one night for some pretty bad seats. And it was cold and then she wanted to go cowboy dancing but i didn't. So i walked home all sad and sat in the sauna. On the walk home is when i smelled summer (next page), so that was nice.

Then a few days later Shilo and i snuck into the last events. The barrel racing and bull riding were awesome. Shilo said she was probably the only kid who got to sneak in with her dad.

CHIEF JOSEPH DAYS
54TH ANNUAL PRCA RODEO
NO REFUNDS
SATURDAY UNCOVERED RES
JULY 24, 1999 -7:00
E
Row/Box
N.U.C12
Sect

89

Today i was stopped in the middle of this road. I was busy hurrying along under an almost full moon. The sun had just gone over the western hills. A gust of sweet summer air hit me in the face and for just a few split-up seconds i could feel the WHOLE ENTIRE summerness. And not just there going up that hill smelling all of just-rained-on pavement and newly baled hay, but I mean the ALL of summer everywhere on this weather-beaten planet. Every activity and human experience that occurs with the coming of this season of warmness, tall grass, pot lucks, and plunges in cold lakes. For just a moment i met summer and felt its bliss, I'll never forget that moment.

90

the day we drew

the clouds and ate the purple heads off the clovers in the field behind the house. We also

fell to sleep in the middle of the day after mowing the lawn.

when we awoke we didn't know where we were.

Shane kept talking about getting his hair cut this week, so i took him into Don Martin's old-style barber shop for a nice trim. Shane is at the age now (13) where he is thinking lots about his looks. Back when he was younger he didn't worry about such things.

BUZZZZZZ

THE
DAY
THE
RAINS
CAME

So now Shane looks about like this

He said that the guy made it way too short.

92

SOME THINGS THAT FUEL MY CREATIVITY

the full moon

mmmmmmm

those small wrapped-up caramels

MILK MAID

MILK MADE

Good Books (SID-HA-THA)

really pretty girls

Red Fezzes

JUST EVERYTHING!!

other people's drawing journals

Big Flowers

Little Bugs

Butter Flies

Andrew Wyeth's paintings

HOW ABOUT YOU?

93

In this hot summer day, 300 bike riders rode into our little town and set up a tent village up on the hill at the High School. I absolutely love tents and biker people are pretty cool too, so i went up to check it out. Got talking to Dave who had an ice pack on his sore foot. He said the group was called THE OREGON BICYCLE RIDE, which sounded kind of boring, i mean couldn't they have called it the GREAT or GRAND or something bicycle ride? Anyway for the last 13 years a big bunch of pedalers rides across the state for a 7-day ride and they stop in all the hick towns along the way and swap howdees with us locals.

JOSEPH HIGH

DAVE

94

TWO-DAY DRIVE to pick UP THE KIDS

Driving across the state to pick up the kids today. Stopped in the town of Fox and drew the old church. Swung with bare feet high into a warm blue sky at the school playground across the street, Just feeling like birds do, swushing the dusty ground, then upward through the brightness. Earlier in the day i waded knee deep in a stream and became a fish there in the cool, dark, rocky shadows.

BIRDS
FISH
BLUE
HEAVEN
SKY

* the wind blowing thru the old swing-set tubes at the school sound like a drunken organ...

95

Near the southern end of the John Day Valley is a town called Dayville. The antique store there is known far and wide for it's amazing collection. I stopped in and took a tour, running fast across the hot main street in my still bare

on a and items. Before my head all sprinkler. A had a sign on "23 FEET early '50s

feet. Sat out lawn bench drew a few leaving i got soaked in the big oak tree it that said AROUND." An Ford sedan sat on the edge of town for sale. Up the road i saw 6 brand new birdhouses all clustered on a tall wooden pole. Swam in the John Day River near the Fossil Beds.

milk can

garden weeder

Opps! DREW THIS PAGE UP SIDE DOWN.

DAYVILLE OR 97825 USPS JUL 26 1999

96

WALTON LAKE

Met the kids and cousins in the hot desert city of Prineville. They were all tan and happy and saying what a great time they'd had. Then we all drove 25 miles into a nearby forest to camp overnight at this lake. The girls swam before sundown. We saw baby ducks.

SUNNY 75°

97

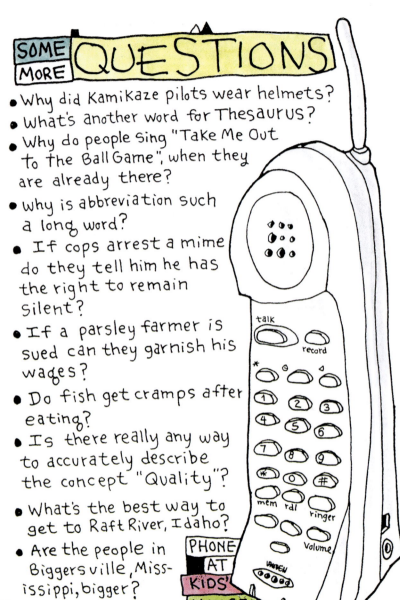

- Why did Kamikaze pilots wear helmets?
- What's another word for Thesaurus?
- Why do people sing "Take Me Out to the Ball Game", when they are already there?
- Why is abbreviation such a long word?
- If cops arrest a mime do they tell him he has the right to remain silent?
- If a parsley farmer is sued can they garnish his wages?
- Do fish get cramps after eating?
- Is there really any way to accurately describe the concept "Quality"?
- What's the best way to get to Raft River, Idaho?
- Are the people in Biggersville, Mississippi, bigger?

talk
record
*
1 2 3
4 5 6
7 8 9
* 0 #
mem rdl ringer
Volume
UNIDEN

PHONE
AT
KIDS'
HOUSE

98

WALLOWA LAKE KARTS
259592
259592
$4.00 $6.00
INDIANA TICKET

Shane boy racing thru the cones and doing an evening paddle at the lake one summer evening.

Somedays are so busy i only get to stop and draw one or two things. Somedays nothing at all...

unidentified frying object

WHAT WE DID ON OUR SUMMER VACATION

AUGUST 16TH

It's near the end of summer. Lynne has a whopping 10 days off and we are heading for the Oregon Coast to play in the waves. The first day we left home around 4PM and only got as far as the parents' house 80 miles away. We saw a movie in town and slept beneath howling coyotes on the hill.

101

One place that i forgot to tell you about is the stop we made in the tiny town of Mabton, Washington. That's where Lynne's mother was buried 3 years ago after she passed away from a sudden heart attack.

It was all sunny and hot as we drove thru the deserted streets and dilapidated old red brick buildings. The only place that looked taken care of was the bank building surrounded by flowers. We went barefoot into the grocery store for water and popsicles. Lynne said she used to have banana popsicles when they would come here to visit her great grandmother years ago.

The cemetery is on the edge of town next to a smelly dairy farm. We went in, parked the car, and sat for a long time next to her tombstone that reads BELOVED GRANDMOTHER. Dogs were off in the distance barking. A set of cold aluminum sprinklers went chit, chit, chit nearby. And the wind blew on all the strange-shaped bushes and trees. Lynne only cried once while cleaning off the marker. I think she has accepted that her mother is away now for a very long time.

102

Lynne woke up this morning at 7AM. She said, "Maybe we should be getting the kids up early so they get used to the school hours coming up!"

We think it's pretty weird to be camping in a crowded campground and having all these neighbors that you don't even talk to. You sort of pretend that they aren't really there, when actually they are. Usually we camp all by ourselves in remote places.

Lynne's really big tent ↓

girl in next campsite in sleeping bag ↓

The beach at this park is covered with small flat rocks. Every time we come here we get a sack full and take them all the way home, clear across the state to a place they've never been before. Then we stack them in little piles.

103

Today we threw all our stuff in the car, drew in some deep breaths of all that special desert air, and drove to the coast. And it was a long way, so there was plenty of time to think about stuff and

GUY WHO GASSED UP THE CAR IN THE DALLES

CHOCOLATE SO GOOD IT'S SCARY

for Lynne's sleeping pad to come loose and fly off the top of the car! And i thought about what a unique family experience it is to go out on a vacation. First of all you're in a small space travelling along and everyone talks to each other for hours on end. And sometimes it can get real quiet or maybe someone's feelings get hurt from all that joking, but for our family it's almost always an amazing feeling of gettingalongness and happiness that fills the car. And i was wondering, aren't most kids on a trip fighting and arguing all day? So it's a real nice experience 'cause when you're all back at home, everyone's always going a million different directions and there's all this unconnectedness and feelings of being alone with all those thoughts.

GUY IN FRONT OF US AT GROCERY STORE

OUR FAVORITE SNACK LIME-FLAVORED CHIPS

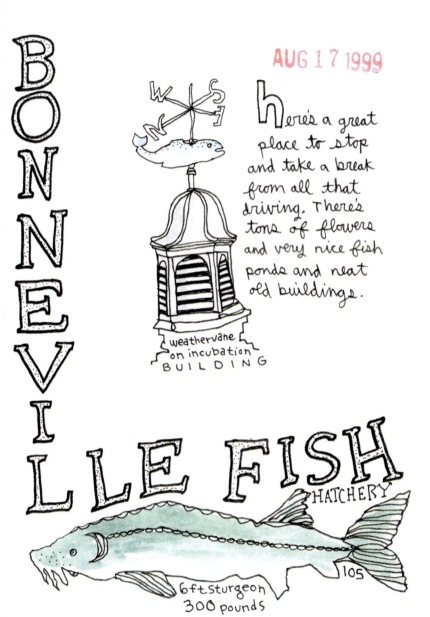

BONNEVILLE

Here's a great place to stop and take a break from all that driving. There's tons of flowers and very nice fish ponds and neat old buildings.

weathervane
on incubation
BUILDING

LLE FISH
HATCHERY

6 ft. sturgeon
300 pounds

105

AUG 18 1999

It's been 3, maybe even 4 years since we've been to the coast and within minutes both kids are in the waves. Lynne is right in there too, prowling around with a camera to her eye, getting shots of them leaping and screaming in the cold salty water. I'm quite content sitting on the sand trying to "capture the moment", as they say. Several times Lynne comes over to lure me in but i say no, no, and no three times. Then she brings the camera to me, runs screaming into the water, and holds the kids' hands as they back further and further into the waves. Pretty soon the whole gang comes over, shivering, covered in goosebumps and stands around asking each other if they're cold. I am perfectly dry and crunch the gritty sand between my big toes.

106

sand ↑
dollar

Sand ↑

CALIFORNIA #4435 Lg PLUM

SHILO BOUGHT ONE OF THOSE NEW GREEN PLUMS

RUBBER STAMP

CASTLE BUILDERS

Day two at the beach was cloudy and cold. We slept in. Took a walk on the beach. Shilo counted 61 dead birds. Sat around the cedarwood campfire, then took a scenic drive around the bay in the old Dodge. We caught baby crabs, watched boogie boarders in the surf, and wondered what it would be like to live out here on the coast in all this fogginess and damp weather. If you lived here you would just forget about having a tan. And your clothes would always feel soggy. And campfires wouldn't burn. Mostly they just smoke and get in your eyes. But maybe you'd get used to all that stuff.

OCEANSIDE OR 97134
AUG 19 1999
USPS

BABY CRAB FOUND IN THE BAY

THE ARCHES AT OCEAN SIDE

A GUY, HIS WIFE, AND A BABY CHECKING CRAB POTS

107

I was so busy drawing this that I didn't get a chance to climb the stairs to see the polished prism glass.

CAPE MEARES lighthouse

GIFT SHOP

108

AUG 20 1999

ODDS and ENDS

LADY SMOKING IN BIG WINTER JACKET IN TILLAMOOK

FIRESTARTER MADE FROM CARDBOARD CHIPS AND WAX

SHILO'S RING THAT GOT SMISHED IN HER SHOE THEN I MADE IT ALL STRAIGHT AGAIN WITH THE PLIERS

DAY FOUR

Cape Meares Light House

SHILO'S HAIR SPRAY THAT SPRAYED ALL OVER HER MAKE-UP KIT THAT I LAID A HEAVY BAG ON

ha spr

OLD SPRUCE TREE NEAR OUR CAMP-SITE

109

LAST DAY on the BEACH

On the third day we rose from our fluffy down bags to blue sky and a light southern breeze. There were ashes from last night's fire on everything in camp. Before long we were on the beach with a shovel, pan, and cup to build a drip castle at the water's edge. Kids were running through the ankle-deep water. Dogs were barking and barking and chasing balls into the surf. An older couple rode by on new bicycles with a white poodle in one of their baskets. A young couple walked by arm in arm, wearing sandals, billowing plaid shirts, and scrunchy caps. It made me think of Shilo in the near future. How i hope she finds a really neat guy. One who will be so good to her and help her to lead a happy LIFE.

AUG 19 1998

110

SUNNY
WARM
ONE
CLOUD

We found some amazing small pebbly sand here at Fogarty Beach. And lots of agates. We watched the sun go down over the blue-black Pacific. Then a lady in a yellow shirt and red hat walked down those stairs in the drawing and fed some bread to about 30 seagulls. When we got back to the car a state policeman had given our car a $61 parking ticket!

$70
A
NIGHT

SOME
NEAT
OLD
THINGS
IN
OUR
MOTEL
ROOM

SHOPPING SPREE

SHANE'S SILVER TAB PANTS

You know there's all kinds of degrees of pampering in this world. I just finished a book called <u>CAMP TEN</u>. It's about Yosemite rock climbing in the early years. These guys were so tough that they'd sleep on rock ledges with only their clothes for protection. On one climb Galen Rowell showed up with a pad and sleeping bag and was called a "camper!"

These days it seems that my two kids and their mom would like nothing better than to go shopping. I on the other hand hate to buy stuff and have begun calling them "shoppers!" whenever they come home with all those consumer goods. Today they dragged me screaming into the Gap. But i must confess, i found a pretty cool pair of pants.

SHILO'S MESSENGER BAG PURSE

DAN'S YELLOW LONG-SLEEVED SHIRT

LYNNE'S SIZE ONE DRESS PANTS

112

After that big shopping spree we drove from the cool air of the coast on into the inland heat and traffic jams of a friday evening, all the way to Grandad's house. We ate a huge dinner out, then played with a

LAST DAY of VACATION

big beach ball in the front yard. Took a long walk the next morning and found a new golf ball. Sat to draw the garage and the neighbor's house from a chair in the backyard. It's really amazing how close the houses are here. You can hear the people next door sneeze.

113

HOMEWARD·BOUND ::

Lynne said she wanted to drive so i crawled in the
back seat with all my drawing stuff and sat
with Shilo, who was writing in her journal.
And at first it felt weird to not have to be the
one watching the road, but after awhile i just got
all laid back and comfortable with my feet out
the window and wind on my face and just watched
all that passing scenery as it reeled on by.

We are all pretty sure we had a good trip and
everyone's glad to be home in their own big
beds. There are clothes to wash and telephone
messages to check and the lawn's grown up like
some jungle. 16 eggs were in the henhouse and
there's lots of   fresh green lettuce in
the garden. And all   the cats wander out
and follow us   around the yard. And
like typical cats   they act like they
could care less that   we were back home.

the NEW WILLOW LOUNGE CHAIR

BACK FRAME

SIDEVIEW

that i built last summer. First i went to talk with master chair builder Greg about the weird design. He said it would probably work if i used slightly bowed pieces for the back rest part. That way it would be more comfortable to sit in. So i gathered all the red willow wood from along the river here by the drawing studio. Then i cheated some. Don't tell Greg but i held the bent part on the frame with 2 wires then nailed it to the deck before applying all those cross pieces. Now i can sit in the morning light to listen to the birds or the big river sounds.

115

For those of you readers who have never read any previous versions of these Chronicles, here is a look at the homemade studio that i like

to stay and work in most of the time when not travelling

the SAUNA about. The sauna is much like an Indian sweat lodge and leaves you feeling deeply cleaned and relaxed. 😊

117

And here's a few more pictures of my 14-year-old boy Shane. He and I were busy one summer day carving our walking sticks on the studio porch. We sold them in a local store.

One morning we were camped out somewhere and i got a shot of him sleeping. The sun was just coming up and was creating cool silhouettes of grass and weeds on the wall....

119

I always get mad at myself for awhile when i get out forgot to bring. Late last night after driving the sweet-smelling desert of Nevada, i stumb amongst ghostly white rocks, loose sand, and som sticker bushes to set up the tent along the lapping sh had forgotten my headlamp. And the other thing i left of hectic departure was a washcloth and towel which lakes and streams.

I needed to take this trip to meet with an old frier company is thinking about putting my drawings on ca Yesterday was very nice. The old Dodge was all tune journey and just slid on down the road. Big hay us around on Hwy. 80. A sleek black Mercedes clouds of smoke then came to a halt on stretch of Hwy 95. I stopped and rode n bike thru the alkaline desert and watched go down at 7.

120

CRUISE

WALKER LAKE 6AM

trip and realize the things i
hours from Oregon and down thru
ru the darkness
ckly
this big lake. I
hind in that incredible flurry
me in handy when bathing in

Los Angeles, whose
d other products.
for this 3,000 mile
ucks buffeted
ewed huge
nely
w
h

← ducks that
would dive
under the
water for
over one
minute.

ELEV. 4,084

121

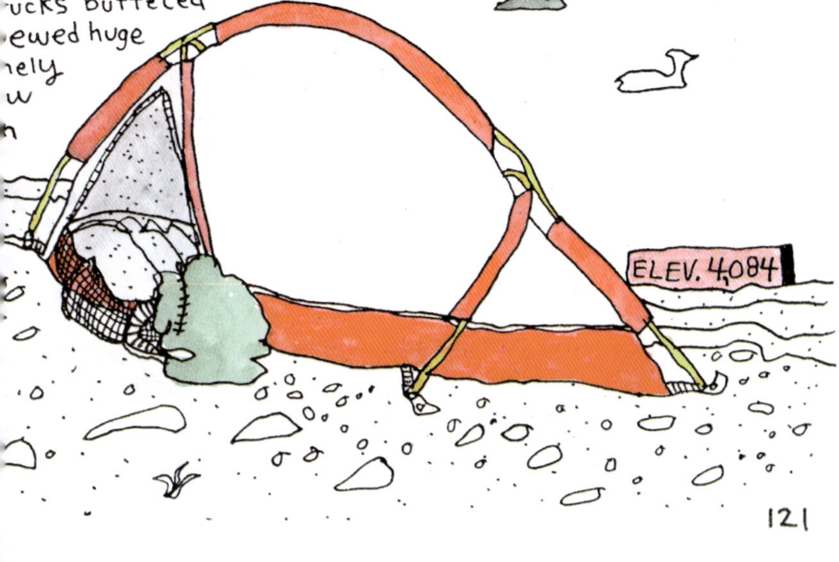

YOSEMITE

Yosemite National Park

SEP·09·99

Yosemite, CA

employee
housing at
Tuolumne
meadows

the view from Olmsted point looking south

flowers
found in
the ditch
at the
INSPIRATION
POINT
overlook

The next
morning i
took a detour
from my custom-
ary path and turned right at Mono
Lake to finally see Yosemite Park.
The road goes right up and up and finally over 10,000 ft Tioga Pass. And i don't
know if i've ever even written the word
spectacular before but that's what kept
coming to mind over and over again.

WELCOME TO YOSEMITE
TIOGA PASS ENTRANCE
CASH $20.00

122

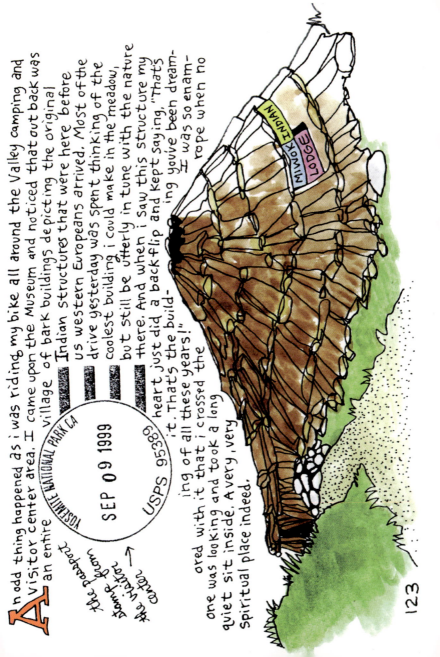

An odd thing happened as i was riding my bike all around the Valley camping and Visitor center area. I came upon the Museum and noticed that out back was an entire village of bark buildings depicting the original Indian structures that were here before us western Europeans arrived. Most of the drive yesterday was spent thinking of the coolest building i could make in the meadow, but still be utterly in tune with the nature there. And when i saw this structure my heart just did a backflip and kept saying, "That's it. that's the build-ing you've been dream-ing of all these years!" I was so enam-ored with it that i crossed the one was looking and took a long quiet sit inside. A very, very Spiritual place indeed.

the passport stamp from the water canyon →

YOSEMITE NATIONAL PARK CA

SEP 09 1999

USPS 95389

INDIAN
MIWOK
LODGE

123

That meeting in Los Angeles was beckoning so i headed out of the valley in the soft evening rain, stopping only once at the base of El Capitan to strain my neck and eyes to see the ant-like climbers far above. Drove all the way down the winding road and into the hot flatlands, thru the town of Fresno, which probably looked a whole bunch different than when a young Woody Guthrie blasted thru on a boxcar back in the '40s. Driving, driving, further south till i finally pooped out at a cheap motel at a crossroads and fell to sleep watching some old war movie on the black and white channel.

Up early the next morning i talked about Dodge cars with a cussing old truck driver before catching the freeway south. Gassed up at a little oasis called Grapevine, then drove into the teaming masses of L.A. Only got lost once, had an interesting meeting and wonderful lunch with Alex and Brad, then headed for those glorious Sierra Mountains.

SEP 10 1999

After getting lost in the twilight on a bicycle ride in the Alabama Hills above Lone Pine i slept in the tent among the rocks. Up at the Whitney Portal campground the next morning i bumped into an old friend and we spent most of the afternoon climbing the highest mountain in the lower 48 states.

124

fter soaking my tired self in Hot Creek near Mammoth Mountain i drove the old car into the pine trees, past a NO CAMPING sign and spent

SEP 11 1999

an absolutely silent night under the stars on dry and crackling pine needles. The next day i got to ride my bike all over the ski mountain on a nice wide, sandy trail. It is a neat way to see the area when all the snow is gone away.

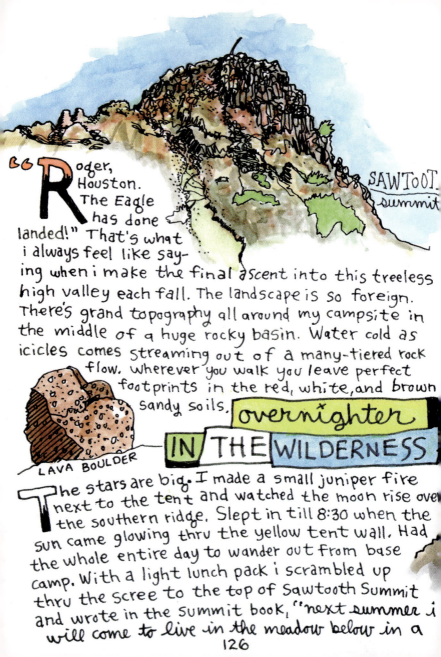

SAWTOOTH summit

"**R**oger, Houston. The Eagle has done landed!" That's what i always feel like saying when i make the final ascent into this treeless high valley each fall. The landscape is so foreign. There's grand topography all around my campsite in the middle of a huge rocky basin. Water cold as icicles comes streaming out of a many-tiered rock flow. Wherever you walk you leave perfect footprints in the red, white, and brown sandy soils.

LAVA BOULDER

overnighter IN THE WILDERNESS

The stars are big. I made a small juniper fire next to the tent and watched the moon rise over the southern ridge. Slept in till 8:30 when the sun came glowing thru the yellow tent wall. Had the whole entire day to wander out from base camp. With a light lunch pack i scrambled up thru the scree to the top of Sawtooth Summit and wrote in the summit book, "next summer i will come to live in the meadow below in a

aspen LEAF

SIERRA
DESIGNS
DIVINE
LIGHTNING

THE TWO-POUND TENT

little tipi. Then i will finally be free..." From the summit i headed west and went up and down for the next 3 hours, looking at odd rocks and following animal trails while dreaming of what i would do if i could stay in that wonderland for a week, or 2 weeks, or even a month. And because there'd be no phone, no mail, no noise, and no people, i think mostly I'd have to just learn to do nothing. Which would be a hard thing to do....

TWIN peaks

don't know if you know about a book i had published recently. It's called <u>HOW TO MAKE A JOURNAL OF YOUR LIFE</u> and i got to travel up to Spokane for a book fair signing. It was held at the convention center on the old EXPO grounds. Spokane is a wonderful city filled with old brick buildings, a river and waterfall and a homey bookstore called Aunties. I rode my bike all over the place, had dinner out with the publicist Rachel and some book reps, signed books in the city park and slept up on the hill under a bright full moon.

SPOKANE
CLOCK
TOWER
9.99

128

the PALOUSE COUNTRY

the newly plowed wheat fields near Spokane. They
call this the Palouse country. Yesterday a huge
dust storm blew thru and caused a 50-car accident.
Now the air is all clean and clear from a
recent rain. I stopped the car near an
old farm and
drew the
furrows
in the fields.
The brown hills look
like the top of a frosted
chocolate cake.

129

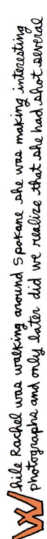

While Rachel was walking around Spokane she was making interesting photographs and only later did we realize that she had shot several

pictures of the chrome parts of my car! Also during the bookfair i saw the author Sherman Alexie and wanted to go up and meet him but was too shy. I did stand nearby though and listened as he talked and

laughed with a guy. They were talking about how back in college the devil was their best friend. then they laughed some more. I think it had something to do with the old college drinking days maybe......

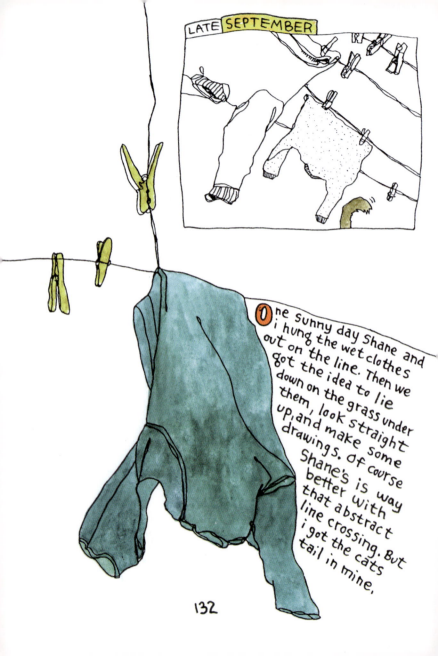

One sunny day Shane and i hung the wet clothes out on the line. Then we got the idea to lie down on the grass under them, look straight up, and make some drawings. of course Shane's is way better with that abstract line crossing. But i got the cats tail in mine,

132

Have you noticed how high tech the outdoor equipment world has become? $400-dollar jackets, hydration systems, and enough goose down in one sleeping bag to keep you warm at minus 20° F! There's naked geese out there somewhere!

GARMONT

X CRIVEL Y

133

A QUIET BOOK DAY

"I was always a big hand to walk along and look at the things along the side of the road. Too curious to stand and wait for a ride. Too nervous to set down and rest. Too struck with the traveling fever to wait. While the other long strings of hitch-hikers was taking it easy in the shade back in the town, I'd be tugging and walking myself to death over the curves, wondering what was just around the next bend; walking to see some distant object, which turned out to be just a big rock, or knoll, from which you could see and wonder about other distant objects. Blisters on your feet, shoes hot as a horse's hide. Still tearing along. I covered about fifteen miles of country, and finally got so tired that I walked out to one side of the road, laid down in the sun, and went off to sleep. I woke up every time a car slid down the highway, and listened to the hot tires sing off a song, and wondered if I didn't miss a good, easy, cool ride all of the way into California."————— Woody Guthrie
BOUND FOR GLORY

EARLY FALL

Sometimes the kids and i sit on the living room floor all evening with the stereo cranked up high and we draw all sorts of neat things we find in magazines and books. It is a neat way to spend time together.

AUDUBON

135

The world has become lovelier. I am alone, and I don't suffer from my loneliness. I don't want life to be anything other than what it is. I am ready to let myself be baked in the sun till I am done. I am eager to ripen. I am ready to die, ready to be born again.

* * *

All of us wanderers are made like this. A good part of our wandering and homelessness is love, eroticism. The romanticism of wandering, at least half of it, is nothing else but a kind of eagerness for adventure. But the other half is another eagerness—an unconscious drive to transfigure and dissolve the erotic. We wanderers are very cunning—we develop those feelings which are impossible to fulfill; and the love which actually should belong to a woman, we lightly scatter among small towns and mountains, lakes and valleys, children by the side of the road.   * * *

Where am I going to sleep tonight? Who cares! What is the world doing? Have new gods been discovered, new laws, new freedoms? Who cares! But up here a primrose is blossoming and bearing silver fuzz on its leaves, and the light sweet wind is singing below me in the poplars, and between my eyes and heaven a dark golden bee is hovering and humming—I care about that. It is humming the song of happiness, humming the song of eternity. Its song is my history of the world.

from **Wandering**
by HERMANN HESSE

136

Last week i was up in the Wilderness, high above our valley of small towns. And as i sat way up there looking down i traced all the many roads and trails i had travelled over the last ten years. Some days I'll travel the six miles between the kids' & my house several times a day. And from that height i could see practically the entire county. And as i ran my eyes up and down all those routes i had travelled, i began to speed it up like one of those fast-motion films of a street scene where the cars and people go zooming all around, back and forth, and the clouds and even the sun go quickly across the sky. And within just a short while i figured i had probably retraced all the travelling i had done here. But what was most surprising of all was to look out beyond the roads and paths and see how much of the land i had never set foot on or seen. All that movement had been confined to a predetermined route. A 60 m.p.h. blur from point A to B. I'm always thinking about all those other neat places right here in this county that I'd like to walk and see and discover.

This is the new moon that looks like a clipped finger-nail, up in the western sky at 6 PM tonight.

This is one of those large-style farm tractors.

OCT 13 1999

SKETCHES i mAde todaY

This is the old juniper post Shane and i found in a cow pasture and my antique rake.

This is a light pole at the place where i was waiting for Shane and his mom this morning.

This one is of Shane. He is eating on one of his favorite foods. A cheese and ham dinner roll.

138

Here is a small drawing i made last weekend. I was camped out on the lakeshore and ended up sitting there on the beach for the whole entire day. Well except for when i rode the bike up to the marina to see if someone there had towed our old aluminum canoe into the dock, thinking it was a rental. All summer long, we had just left it pulled up by our campsite and then one day it was gone.

Round about noon is when i saw these two old boys come trolling slowly by. I imagined that they just couldn't think of anything else to do that day so they drove up to the lake and went fishing. And they were quite even possibly boyhood friends who used to do the same thing years and years ago. I could see them walking up streams and sitting at the lake's edge with a sack of food and jars of fish eggs in their pockets. Then again they might have just met each other at a senior citizen luncheon...

STILL MISSING one slightly dinged-up old silver canoe

139

DRAWING

is one of the easiest ways to get in touch with your silent spirit. If you just let your pen go on its own accord & see the line that it makes, you will know moments of true freedom and absolute bliss. You will also know why it is that hobos never do go home. You will finally understand why all those fishermen stand for hours on the edge of lonely streams.

MAYAN

SKUNK

FISHERMAN

140

"The man who sat on the ground in his tipi meditating on life and its meaning, accepting the kinship of all creatures and acknowledging unity with the universe of things, was infusing into his being the true essence of civilization." CHIEF LUTHER STANDING BEAR

TEA STRAINER

I have enjoyed reading these and other good thoughts out of the book TOUCH THE EARTH by T.C. McLuhan. I like to learn of other ideas from people like myself who have spent many years searching for the supposed "secret to life." What is it that would finally end the search and make us all more content, less confused, and at peace?

Many of us have done all kinds of difficult soul searching. We have done lots of mind twists to try and think new and different thoughts. We've taken classes, studied theories, and all to what end? Has it made us any wiser? Has all that restless activity made us feel more WHOLE or HAPPIER? After reading quotes like this one above i realize there is no reason for all the wondering. That for me all i need to do is draw the whole world. Bliss really is that close. What am i waiting for?

JEL

141

BROOKLYN

Old beat streets with broken-
down apartment houses and
back lot grease pits
for car repair.

On a dusky friday morning i got
on the L train and rode under the
East River to Brooklyn to meet up
with and draw with Johanna.

Someone
threw
a pair
of bots
on the
electric
line at maujer
and lorimer st S.

KID WALKING DOWN STREET W/HANDS IN PANTS!

NYC

DAN'S

FISH

SILVER
AND
BLACK
HYDRANT

ROSY the CAT
at Johanna's...

hey look at these drawings that were made on a
trip to New York City last year. I wasn't getting
much published that year so i started to make a set of
new sketchbooks called DRAW. In the year's time
i filled about 12 books.
142

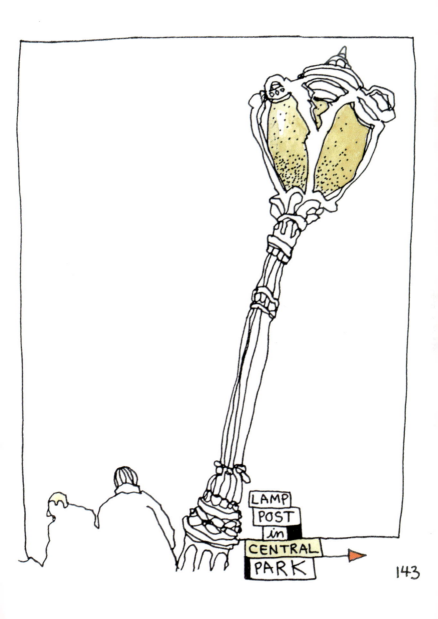

LAMP
POST
in
CENTRAL
PARK

143

*A friend loaned me a bike, which proved to be a really great way to see the city.

I think it would be very cool to be a traveller via bicycle. They are very easy to maneuver into narrow streets. When i get back home maybe I'll go do some hobo biking around. To be out drawing everyday is a wonderful way to become humble and to praise the whole world. While

L I T T L E
I T A L Y

drawing this window as i sat in the shade on a stoop, i could see a flock of pigeons flying high above in the sunshine. They were being reflected in the window of a nearby car. People were not being very friendly today. Except for that waitress in Brooklyn. She was nice. I only have 75¢ in my pockets now.

144

END
NYC

Just the other day i was having these thoughts about how everyone seems to be absorbing all the hyped-up cultural noise nowadays of T.V., music and radio news, magazines, and computers.

CASSADY
NEAL
DENVER
26362

And how that can clutter up a mind so thoroughly that a person can reach the age of 20 or even 40 and hardly have had any original and personal thoughts of their own.

Then Shane came home from school with an assignment to write a paper about why kids have to go to school. It was titled "COMPULSORY EDUCATION" and here is the last paragraph of it that we wrote together. "I would rather have more time to listen to my own thoughts and ideas so i can find out who i really am and what I'm going to spend my life doing. Instead of having teachers, T.V., and the Internet fill me with more and more and more information that i probably will never

use anyway."

SHANE
age 14

145

"....he drew little pic-
tures, and once he made
a sketch of his friend
to amuse him...." CARSON
McCULLERS

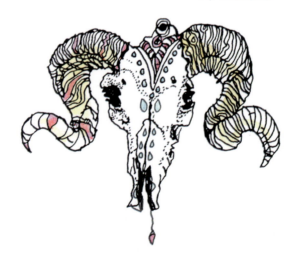

146

I am now seeing that this is the last story page, which does make me feel quite sad. It's been real nice to talk with you and hopefully we will continue our conversation soon. I'll leave you with a few quiet lines written one day long ago: See the sun? It's going down, down over the busy town. See the clouds turn to peach and pumpkin orange? They're heading east very slowly. Like a big ship sailing over treetops, buildings, grass, bugs, asphalt, and sad quiet people. Only the birds are rejoicing, clapping their soft wings as they lead the ship eastwards.....

d.price

a niece's BLUE RIBBON hog at the fair.

Developing runner bean

"I begun to pace back and forth, keeping my gaze out the window, way down, watching the diapers and underwear blow from fire escapes and clothes lines on the back sides of the buildings; seeing the smoke whip itself into a hazy blur that smeared across the sky and mixed in with all of the other smoke that tried to hide the town. Limp papers whipped and beat upwards, rose into the air and fell head over heels, curving over backwards and sideways, over and over, loose sheets of newspaper with pictures of people and stories of people printed somewhere on them, turning loops in the air. And it was blow little paper, blow! Twist and turn and stay up as long as you can, and when you come down, come down on a pent-house porch, come down easy so's not to hurt your self. Come down and lay there in the rain and the wind and the soot and smoke and the grit that gets in your eyes in the big city—and lay there in the sun and get faded and rotten. But keep on trying to tell your message, and keep on trying to be a picture of a man, because without that story and without that message printed on you there, you wouldn't be much. Remember, it's just maybe, some day, sometime, somebody will pick you up and look at your picture and read your message, and carry you in his pocket, and lay you on his shelf, and burn you in his stove. But he'll have your message in his head and he'll talk it and it'll get around. I'm blowing, and just as wild and whirling as you are, and lots of times I've been picked up, throwed down, and picked up; but my eyes has been my camera taking pictures of the world and my songs has been messages that I tried to scatter across the back sides and along the steps of the fire escapes and on the window sills and through the dark halls."

148

BOUND FOR GLORY

woody guthrie

© Doug Biggert photo

Moonlight Chronicles.

author d. price has been studying his secrets & dreams since escaping from high school in 1975. He is currently a father, lettuce and carrot grower, snowboarding hobo, sauna and sun-lover, river inner-tuber, world wanderer and journal maker and a fully licensed, card carrying KID, who listens only to his intuition and who has lived in a tent by secluded riverbanks with deer, who he believes he must have descended from in a past life. Most folks are pretty sure he's nuts. You can find out for yourself by writing him at HOBO HILL • BOX 109 JOSEPH • OR • 97846 or www.MOONLIGHTCHRONICLES.com

149

CHRONICLE

All us scribes on the friendly planet earth promise to continue our sketching ways. On that endless search for TRUTH and BEAUTY.

To take long sabbaticals from our busy lives. To live in a simple fashion and be close to NATURE. To honor our every breath and give huge thanks for good health, lots of art supplies, and Shilo's cookies. To truly believe that LESS is MORE, but to have an old car because we love to travel and be FREE. We pledge to DRAW and WRITE each day. To be silent and watch bugs. To count stars and ride on clouds and to always study REALITY. Oh, and to eat lots of natural food and to only occasionally wear those darn shoes....

CREED

* all drawings and text created with SAKURA pens. www.gellyroll.com